© 2009 Lincolnshire Vintage Vehicle Society Ltd

Published by Venture Publications Ltd on behalf of the

ISBN 978 1905 304 295

Computer Origination, Design and Layout by John A Senior

WHEN OUR LIONS LIVED IN JERSEY

In August 1959, my parents and I spent a holiday in Jersey. We flew from London Airport (as Heathrow was then) in a Dakota DC3. It was rather a bumpy ride; my mother vowed she would never fly again once she returned home and she never did.

The uncomfortable flight was worth it, though, and we had a marvellous holiday, making our way round the island by Jersey Motor Transport bus. The majority of the vehicles we used were post-war single-deckers, but of course JMT was well known amongst enthusiasts (the relatively few of us that there were in those days) for its unrivalled collection of ancient Leylands.

There were varieties of pre-war Titans, Tigers, Lions and Cubs still in service, but behind the depot at Snow Hill was a dream-like collection of even older Leylands, withdrawn and mouldering in the summer sun, awaiting their fate. Although I had only a Brownie 127 camera then (with 8 frames to a film, and films were expensive from pocket money), I managed to photograph quite a few, including the ex-West Yorkshire PLSC1 and ex-Lancashire United LT1 Lions which were lucky enough to be rescued by the fledgling LVVS.

They are thankfully still very much with us 50 years on and I have been delighted to renew my acquaintance with them since our retirement to (where else but) Lincoln.

Peter Wilks

FOREWORD

Nowadays the restoration, display and active use of historic vehicles is big business, with examples of all shapes, sizes and descriptions being regularly seen on Britain's roads. Some vehicles are privately owned and cared for, whilst others are kept in museums such as ours, of which there are now quite a number throughout the UK. The general public can also not only admire the transport of yesteryear at countless rallies and events put on throughout the country during the year, but can now often enjoy riding on these fine vehicles at 'running' days.

All terrific stuff, but it wasn't always like this and fifty years ago it was perhaps looked upon with some amusement that a group of old vehicle enthusiasts should get together to purchase four time-expired buses with a view to establishing a road transport museum in the area. But that is what happened in Lincoln in 1959, thanks to the foresight and endeavour of the Society's founding member, Mr Vincent LeTall.

I was delighted when Adrian first suggested that he should write a history of the Society to celebrate its 50th Anniversary in 2009 and chronicle in print just what can

THE LINCOLNSHIRE
VINTAGE VEHICLE SOCIETY

PROGRESS FROM LINCOLN

Founded 1959

New Edition

A group of younger Society members on the upper deck of ex-Lincoln No. 23 circa 1970. Pictured from left to right are Rodney Dimaline, Stuart Howe, David Howe and Adrian Henson.
STEVE MILNER

be achieved when a group of like-minded individuals set about safeguarding our transport heritage for the benefit and enjoyment of future generations.

It has not all been plain sailing by any means, and those of us who have been involved for quite a few years now can certainly reflect upon and remember some lean and worrying times in the Society's history. The Society has become what it is today due to the unstinting efforts of countless individuals and organisations, and the next few years could see further exciting developments on the horizon.

The Society has been very fortunate to have members who have looked upon, cared for and restored the vehicles, as if they were their own. It has also enjoyed strong support from the local councils, our neighbours and businesses in the locality, along with other museums and individuals active in the historic vehicle movement on a national basis.

I know that Adrian has enjoyed the many hours spent researching the material for this publication and I would like to say a big thank you for this record and to all those who have made what has been achieved possible.

Here's to the next 50 years!

Steve Milner
LVVS Chairman

Opposite page: This is, in effect, the third edition of 'Progress From Lincoln', the previous two having appeared in 1969 and 1977 respectively. This was the front cover from the second edition, with a picture of the Ruston Car and the Leyland TD1 bus posed on Pelham Bridge in Lincoln.

Thirty-eight years after taking the photograph opposite, Steve Milner is seen on the steps of the Society's PLSC Lion which took part in the splendid Leyland Centenary event at the National Tramway Museum, Crich.
JOHN A SENIOR

PART 1 –

THE STORY SO FAR

It has often been said that many societies now in existence would never have materialised but for the ideas of one person – and this could not be truer than in the case of the Lincolnshire Vintage Vehicle Society. The person concerned wanted to see how much interest existed in vintage vehicles within the County back in the late nineteen-fifties. At the time the preservation movement was in its infancy; but due to the boundless enthusiasm and endeavour of Mr Vincent LeTall, a small group of like-minded individuals founded what is now the Lincolnshire Vintage Vehicle Society.

Following the Society being mentioned in a local newspaper, 'The Lincolnshire Echo', a well-known local businessman and used commercial vehicle dealer, Sid Twell, contacted the group advising that he had a vehicle which was eminently suitable as a preservation candidate. This turned out to be a 1929 Leyland Lion LT1 bus that had served the public of Lincoln for many years, originally as a service bus and latterly as a snowplough! Its bodywork was also of particular interest, having been built by a local firm, Messrs Applewhite & Co. It was quickly decided that this vehicle would be ideal as the Society's first acquisition and was very generously donated by Mr Twell. In appreciation Sid was offered and was pleased to accept a Vice-Presidency of the Society. This heralded the start of a long and valued association between the Society and the Twell family.

This bus was soon joined by two others built by the same manufacturer. The Society's then President, Mr Herbert Jones, had learnt that Jersey Motor Transport were about to dispose of many of their elderly fleet of buses that they had operated on the Island following acquisition from operators on the mainland. The Society was fortunate to acquire two of their oldest Leyland single-deckers, a 1927 PLSC1 Lion and a 1930 LT1 Lion, at a cost of £40 each plus £40 per vehicle delivery to London docks – a total of £160. Due to the lack of suitable premises at the time the Lincoln Corporation Transport Department kindly provided temporary accommodation for both buses within their bus garage at St Marks.

The initial preoccupation with buses by the Society was soon remedied by the then local MP, Sir Geoffrey de Freitas, who was interested in a very rare make of car which had a strong association with the City. This was the 'Ruston' built by the local company Ruston & Hornsby, but due to the small number produced the possibility of locating a survivor was regarded as rather remote. Before Sir Geoffrey relinquished his seat in Parliament to become British High Commissioner in Ghana he discovered an old Ruston car in Australia and, although it was in a deplorable condition, he arranged for it to be transported back to the UK. Ray Hooley, an LVVS committee member and Librarian at Ruston's at the time, duly contacted Sir Geoffrey and this led to tentative arrangements for the car to be restored through the company. A second survivor was subsequently located at Torpoint in Devon and acquired with the intention of restoring one vehicle from the two, but this one had been adapted for use as a breakdown vehicle and was found

The two Leyland Lions posing outside the former Lincoln Corporation bus garage following their repatriation from Jersey. Vincent LeTall is standing on the steps of the LT1 behind Herbert Jones.
LVVS COLLECTION

The two ex-Jersey Lions and Vincent LeTall's ex-Lincolnshire Leyland Tiger TS7 at an early event – believed to be at the Lincolnshire Showground.
LVVS COLLECTION

The 1920 Ruston 16hp A.1 tourer with Ray Hooley plus the apprentices who carried out the restoration seated in the car.
RAY HOOLEY COLLECTION

to be a different model to the one from Australia. Then, there came news of the auction of 'The Sword Collection' in Scotland, which included another 'Ruston' car. This 1920 model was subsequently acquired by Ruston's in September 1962 and restored to a very high standard by a group of apprentices, passing its MOT test in May 1967. One of the team of apprentices was Pete Francis, who subsequently joined the LVVS; he and his wife Pam went on to become true Society stalwarts. Whilst this fine car is not part of the Society's collection and remains in the care of Siemens Industrial Turbomachinery Ltd, its close association with the LVVS and appearance at Society functions continues to this day.

Mindful of the adage, 'an Englishman's home is his castle', the Society's Management Committee decided that a permanent home should be found and purchased for the growing vehicle collection at the earliest opportunity. A suitable site was soon located just outside the City boundary, totalling three-quarters of an acre of land, and several members generously made loans available so it could be purchased in readiness for the day a permanent

museum could be established. This action as far back as 1962/3 was incredibly far-sighted and has set the Society apart from many other road transport museums around the country by owning its premises.

Acknowledging that a temporary home elsewhere would be required in the meantime, covered accommodation was obtained at the former army headquarters at the Sobraon Barracks on Burton Road in Lincoln. Monday and Wednesday evenings became times when members were invited to come along and work on the vehicles, with night work becoming possible once lighting had been installed and powered by a 'Ruston' stationary engine.

By the time the Society celebrated its fifth birthday in 1964 it was able to reflect, with considerable satisfaction, on the achievements in those first five years of its existence. It had become well-established locally and was rapidly gaining national recognition. The membership was growing steadily and the Society was continually widening its horizons by adding activities such as monthly film shows, outings to places of interest

LINCOLNSHIRE VINTAGE VEHICLE SOCIETY

FOUNDED APRIL, 1959

President :

H. JONES, A.C.C.S.,A.M.INST.T.

What is it all About?

OBJECTS
To secure the preservation of old and interesting vehicles of all types. This is achieved by helping members with the pooling of information, location of spares, provision of working and storage accommodation, and very soon we hope, the founding of a Museum where Vehicles can be on permanent display.

ACTIVITIES
A quarterly Bulletin, the "Con-Rod," issued free to all members, gives details of forthcoming rallies, meetings, items of interest, vehicles for sale and wanted, and progress reports.

REQUIRED
Members with Vehicles (and without, who would like to help with restoration work in their spare time). Members who can help financially and materially with our building programme.

AND OF COURSE

All who have a general interest in our activities.

FURTHER DETAILS
Supplied by contacting Hon. Secretary.

F. V. LETALL, 137 DODDINGTON ROAD, LINCOLN   Phone : 21444

DETAILS OF PROGRESS TO DATE AND A LIST
OF MEMBERS' VEHICLES IS GIVEN OVERLEAF

The 1930 Singer Junior saloon.
JOHN CHILD

plus the attendance of shows and rallies to display the vehicles. Further additions had also been made to the collection. From the heart of the textile country came a unique vehicle, a Leyland Badger single-deck bus, which spent its working life with Bradford Corporation and was used for educational activities up until 1962. This Badger, which was principally a goods chassis, was built in 1930 and carries the oldest Plaxton bus body still in existence. Another interesting vehicle acquired was a 1935 BMMO SOS DON single-deck bus that had been converted into a mobile enquiry office in 1951 for use at Skegness. It was finally retired in 1962 and its owner,

Trent Motor Traction, didn't wish to see it go for scrap. By this time the Society had also been presented with a couple of very interesting cars, a 1930 Singer Junior saloon and a 1936 Standard Flying Twelve.

Lincoln's housing problems in the mid-1960s caused the Society a major headache in 1966, when notice was served that the Sobraon Barracks was to be redeveloped. The Society was therefore faced with the prospect of having nowhere to go other than the bare plot of land purchased some years earlier, with the vehicles parked out in the open and at the mercy of the elements. Fortunately, the City Council came to the Society's

A shot of part of the 'new' Whisby Road premises, before the side extension was added in the late 1970s.
LVVS COLLECTION

7

rescue with a former NAAFI building that was potentially ideal to house the vehicle collection. Negotiations to acquire it were successfully concluded, which then only left the biggest obstacle of all – moving it from its existing location to Whisby Road. In one hectic weekend, with the help and determination of many members, the whole building was moved through the City Centre to the Society's new base. A contractor was then employed to re-erect the main structure and several weekends later the mammoth task of moving the vehicles was undertaken. As many were either undergoing or awaiting restoration most of these had to be towed or transported, including the now famous 1929 all-Leyland Titan TD1 double-deck bus that had been acquired by the Society the previous year.

During this period Society activities continued to develop. In 1966 the Lincolnshire Show was attended for the first time, and this was followed in 1967 by the Society's participation in the London to Brighton run organised by the Historic Commercial Vehicle Club. The 1930 former Lancashire United Leyland Lion LT1 repatriated from Jersey was our principal entry, supported by the 1935 BMMO SOS, which acted as a tender vehicle given the necessity of an overnight stay in Battersea Park. Both of these events went on to become a regular feature in the Society's activities-calendar for many years.

1967 also saw another interesting vehicle arrive at Whisby Road, a 1937 Ford V8 shooting brake, which was placed in our care by the Dowager Countess of Yarborough who had owned it since new. This was followed in the winter of 1967/8 by the City of Lincoln Fire Brigade's old turntable ladder fire appliance, which had given 26 years faithful service. This was yet another

Leyland, and mounted on a TD7 bus chassis, the Merryweather turntable ladder extending to over 100ft. Interestingly, its replacement suffered from a number of teething problems, leading to our appliance seeing a short spell of further active service whilst the replacement was returned to the manufacturers for modifications.

As 1967 drew to a close several improvements were also made to the new Whisby Road premises. The interior walls were lined to safeguard against fire and the weeds inside the building disappeared under a new tarmac floor, making for more pleasant but still very basic working conditions.

1968 saw the first Society Dinner & Dance, and, like other events, it became a regular feature in members' diaries for some years. In May no less than four vehicles took part in the London to Brighton run and at the Lincolnshire Show the Society was formally presented with its first post-war bus by the Managing Director of English Electric Diesels Ltd. This was the 1948 ex-Lincoln Guy Arab III double-decker powered by an experimental Ruston air-cooled diesel engine. It had appeared at the 1948 Commercial Motor Show when new (at the time powered by a Meadows 10.35-litre diesel engine) and following the fitting of its present power unit had endeared itself to the Lincoln travelling public by being heard quite some time before it actually came into view. When first acquired it had to be painted into a different livery to avoid any possible confusion with similar vehicles still in service, the then Society colours of light blue and maroon being chosen as the basis of the colour scheme adopted.

The continuing steady trickle of new arrivals meant that undercover storage was now at a premium, so in 1968/9 two additional buildings were erected at the rear

The ex-Jersey Leyland Lion LT1 plus the 1935 BMMO SOS pictured here setting off from the 'Depot' for the HCVC London to Brighton Run in May 1967.
LVVS COLLECTION

The Ruston car on wedding duty in October 1967 for Pete and Pam Francis.
PAM FRANCIS COLLECTION

A panoramic view of the Society stand at a Lincolnshire Show.
COURTESY OF LINCOLNSHIRE ECHO

The ex-Lincoln Guy Arab being formally presented to the Society at the 1968 Lincolnshire Show.
LVVS COLLECTION

of the premises, one for spares and the other for vehicle storage. The Society is indebted to Sid Twell in providing the steel structures of these buildings.

1969 marked the end of the first decade of the Society, and, to celebrate, an Open Day was held at the premises, with the vehicles parked up along Whisby Road to allow people to take a leisurely amble around them – imagine the chaos that would be caused if this was repeated today. This event has also become a regular in the rally calendar, though in different formats over the years as the surrounding area has been developed. In August the Society attended the first Trans-Pennine run from Manchester to Harrogate, at which the Leyland Lion PLSC1 picked up an award.

1970 was notable for the completion of one of the most ambitious restoration projects ever undertaken by the Society, the 1929 Leyland Titan TD1 double-deck bus originally supplied to Bolton Corporation. After a service life of some 27 years in which it had travelled some 900,000 miles, it was acquired by Leyland Motors who subsequently passed it on to the Society. Much of the body frame had been found to be rotten and had to be replaced. The staircase was also rebuilt to its original open layout, having

One of the additional storage buildings added during 1968/9 under construction, which is now the workshop. The bus just visible is an ex-Lincoln utility Guy acquired for preservation by Cyril Cooke but ultimately found to be beyond redemption.
LVVS COLLECTION

Below: Our first 'Open Day' in 1969.
STEVE MILNER

VEHICLE PROFILE – WH 1553

A 1929 Leyland Titan TD1 with a Leyland lowbridge 51-seat open staircase body

The Leyland TD1 introduced the double-decker to many routes for the first time, as a result of pioneering work by Leyland Motors on a low height design to produce a 'lowbridge' body incorporating an offset sunken gangway upstairs. Lincoln Corporation took delivery of the very first production model as its fleet number 24, FE 9755 in 1927. Our example was supplied new to Bolton Corporation as its fleet number 54 and at a time when the normal life of a bus was about seven years, WH 1553 was a remarkable survivor. In 1936 Bolton Corporation sold it to Hicks of Braintree and the rear platform and staircase were enclosed at some stage during its time with them. In 1947 the bus passed to its last operator, Honeywoods of Stanstead and remained in service until 1956, by which time it had travelled some 900,000 miles! In 1958 this now rare survivor of a truly groundbreaking design was reacquired by Leyland Motors for posterity and they in turn donated it to the Society in 1965. By this time the bus was in relatively poor condition, necessitating the most ambitious and extensive restoration project undertaken in the early years of the Society. Much of the body frame was rotten and had to be replaced, in addition to which the staircase was rebuilt to the original open layout. Newly restored, the bus made its rally debut on the 1970 London to Brighton Run and has since had its seats retrimmed with authentic period moquette.

The TD1, partially stripped down.
LVVS COLLECTION

Going out 'on test' in the summer of 1968.
CYRIL COOKE

The TD1 restored to its former glory.
COURTESY OF LINCOLNSHIRE ECHO

been enclosed during its later working life. For the annual pilgrimage to Brighton that year Society members were joined by members of BBC TV's Blue Peter programme, who travelled on the 1930 Leyland Lion LT1. Later the same month the Society helped with the hosting by the City of Lincoln of members of the Veteran Car Club who were taking part in the 1000 Mile Trial in celebration of the 70th anniversary of this historic event. The original route taken by the pioneers was adhered to wherever possible and, as occurred in the 1900 Run, a lunch stop was made in Lincoln.

Using 1970 as an example, one notable contrast with today's rally calendar is apparent; the season commenced with the London to Brighton run in early May and finished with the Crich Extravaganza at the end of August. 1971 was an exception to this in that at Easter a 'Vintage Commercial Motor Show' was staged in Harrogate at which the newly restored Leyland Titan TD1 and the freshly repainted ex-Jersey Leyland Lion LT1 were exhibited. The same two vehicles also attended the third Trans-Pennine run later that year and provoked some fond memories and story telling amongst Lancashire United Transport employees when parked overnight at that company's Swinton depot.

During the winter of 1971/2 long-delayed work necessary for the Whisby Road premises to be opened as a museum to the general public was completed. The spares collection was sorted and relocated, a sales kiosk was built and the ceiling of the main building was

The TD1 and LT1 plus a party of Society members about to set off on the London to Brighton Run.
LVVS COLLECTION

'ONO', the globetrotting Bristol in 'as acquired' condition.
STEVE MILNER

The AEC Monarch lorry caught here posing for the camera at the 2003 Open Day.
SANDRA RHODES

repainted. The public were admitted for the first time at the annual Open Day held in early June. Later that month the Society also had a film star guesting on the vintage bus service at the Lincolnshire Show; a 1953 Bristol KSW5G double-decker and one of several buses supplied by Sid Twell for use in the 'On The Buses' series of films.

During 1972 the Society acquired another vehicle of celebrity status, a 1949 Bristol K5G double-deck bus. After a relatively uneventful working life 'ONO' was purchased by a group of students and fitted out as a caravan with eight bunks upstairs plus cooking facilities and a sink in the lower saloon. It then journeyed right around the world, was repainted in a red, white and blue Union Jack livery during its travels and suffered various indignities such as colliding with a San Francisco cable-car. Following their return to the UK the students did not wish to see ONO go for scrap, so it passed to the Society for use as a driver training and tender vehicle.

In early 1973 the first car restoration project to be undertaken at Whisby Road was finally completed. This was a 1935 Austin Ten Cabriolet belonging to Mr M Smalec and had taken five years of hard work and great patience. Another significant development at that time was the return of the 1927 Dennis 4-ton lorry, which had been languishing at the rear of the premises since acquisition in 1967, to its original owners, Higgs & Hill. Within a year the company completely restored the vehicle at their Wellingborough depot for use in their centenary celebrations during 1974, returning it to the Society's care the following year.

The Society has generally been prepared to try anything once, and in October 1973 a 'flea market' was held at the premises to try and dispose of some of the surplus spares acquired over the years. The event was moderately successful and has been repeated since, though generally in conjunction with Open Days.

On the restoration front, in autumn 1973 work commenced on ONO to renovate and equip it for its intended function as a tender vehicle. This work continued over the 1974/5 winter and over the 1975/6 winter platform doors were fitted in the light of operational experience. At the same time another group was working on a 1934 AEC Monarch lorry, which had come to the Society in 1968 and upon which work had been at a standstill for some time due to a lack of engine spares. This lorry had spent most of its working life carrying coke and coal supplies to the Bracebridge Mental Hospital at nearby Bracebridge Heath. Restoration was completed in time for the 1975 rally season and the vehicle has been authentically sign written with wording which would not have caused a second glance in its day, but is now seen by some as most inappropriate in today's 'politically correct' age.

In 1977 the 'usual suspects' rallied were joined by a welcome addition and example of our motoring dynasty, a 1932 Austin Seven. This vehicle was kindly loaned to the Society by local businessman Mr J Ruddock and stayed with us for 30 years.

The maturing adolescent years of the Society from 1976 onwards up to its coming of age in 1980 saw some interesting developments in a number of areas. A steady programme of improvements was undertaken on the premises, with three-phase electricity and a compressor being installed in 1977. This was followed by another bay being added to the former NAAFI building between late 1977 and the summer of 1979, with 'community service' workers assisting with some of the work. Several major restoration projects of both Society and members' vehicles were also undertaken at Whisby Road during the period. The ex-Lincoln Ruston-engined Guy bus was treated to a comprehensive mechanical and bodywork refurbishment, and repainted into the livery it carried when its present engine was fitted. Colin Garton went to work on his 1938 AEC Monarch lorry and Dyson trailer, Albert Bratley and his son Mark restored a local 1948 Morris Commercial 30 cwt lorry, Bert Balding did likewise with his 1949 Austin 25 cwt K8 3-way van,

A 1927 Dennis 4-ton lorry

This 4-ton lorry was supplied new to Higgs & Hill Ltd, the body being built in their own workshops. Used continuously in the building trade, it travelled in the region of 250,000 miles before being sold off for £35 in 1942. The Society obtained the vehicle from Smith Clayton Forge in Lincoln in 1967, where it had been used to move castings around the works; its rear springs being replaced by one piece steel beams! Acquired in a very poor state and devoid of some of its original fittings, it was presented to its original owners in 1972, who restored it to 'as new' condition for their centenary celebrations in 1974, before returning it on permanent loan to the Society.

The three views of the Dennis 4-ton lorry show it before, during and after restoration by Higgs & Hill.
LVVS COLLECTION

A shot of the former 'NAAFI' building after the side extension had been added.
LVVS COLLECTION

and the recently acquired ex-Lincoln Corporation 1961 Leyland PD2 double-deck bus was repainted into the 'wrong' livery in which it was originally delivered.

This era was not a time of all-work and no-play though; the Society attended the filming of an episode of a very popular TV show of the time 'Jeux Sans Frontieres' on the Lincolnshire Show Ground in 1978. Having got a taste for showbiz, this was followed up by the Leyland TD1 and the two ex-Jersey Lions being used in a period drama 'Buses', which was shown by the BBC as part of their 'Play for Today' series in March 1980. If this was not enough, the TD1 was also featured by Leyland in promotional material for its new 'Leyland Titan' double-decker. Regular annual events such as the Dinner & Dance, where members could 'boogie' the night away to the delights of the Reverend Kenyon's Church Mice Disco, plus the annual Open Day and Summer Rally also

continued to flourish. Interestingly, in contrast to today, the Annual Rally was then a movable feast, particularly as far as its location was concerned; being held at Mablethorpe in 1977, Belvoir Castle in 1978, followed by Lincoln Cathedral in 1979 and 1980.

1980, the 21st year of the Society, was to prove notable in two key respects, both of which have had a significant bearing on its future development. In late 1979 it had been agreed with the LeTall family that the Society would take responsibility for the 'LeTall Collection', which comprised six buses and five cars. The buses were an open-sided Bedford OB, a Bristol KSW5G, a Bristol LD6B Lodekka, a Chevrolet coach, a Leyland TS7 and a Leyland TD7. The cars comprised two Austin 10s, an Austin 12 tourer, an Austin 16 and an Austin 18. Of these eleven vehicles, all five cars and four of the buses have remained in the Society's care to this day. In May 1980 these fine vehicles were moved from the LeTalls' residence at Ingham to Whisby Road, the ex-Lincoln Leyland TD7 disgracing itself by breaking down on Burton Road en route. These acquisitions were

Vincent LeTall's Leyland TD7 and Leyland TS7 en route from Ingham to Whisby Road.
STEVE MILNER

LINCOLNSHIRE VINTAGE VEHICLE SOCIETY'S

14th. OPEN DAY

THE EVENT OF THE YEAR ~
SUNDAY MAY 17th.1981

at the depot, Whisby Road,
Doddington Road, Lincoln

OPENED OFFICIALLY at 2.00pm. by
MR. TREVOR KNOWLES   MANAGER LINCOLNSHIRE ECHO

Inumerable old cars, buses, motor cycles, commercials, etc.

Browse round the flea market, auto jumble & souvenirs

SUPPORT OUR RAFFLE & HELP THE SOCIETY

REFRESHMENTS
AVAILABLE AT MODERATE PRICES

VEHICLES ARRIVING FROM 11:00 A.M.

ADMISSION
ADULTS 50p
CHILDREN 20p

ENQUIRIES
A.K. HENSON
35, WHARFEDALE ROAD
LONG EATON
NOTTINGHAM   NG 10 3HG
PHONE - LONG EATON 61799

FREE PARKING

Three views of the Society premises taken during the 1980s, the one below including Don Teesdale at work on the Bedford MLD flatbed lorry.
PETER GREY

followed by an even more profound development in November 1980. At an extraordinary general meeting a new constitution was adopted with a view to obtaining charitable trust status, which would mean that the Society and its collection would, in future, be for the benefit of the public and not solely reserved for members.

In early 1981 members were saddened to learn of the death of Sid Twell at the age of 67, a gentleman whose generosity and unfailing support in those early days helped ensure Vincent LeTall's germ of an idea blossomed and grew into what the Society is today.

Looking back, the early 1980s were notable for the level of activity on the broad range of vehicles by now housed at Whisby Road. A number of significant restoration projects were completed, including Dave Gray's Bristol K5G double-deck bus and Steve Milner's AEC Regal single-decker. Ken Allen made steady progress with his Morris 10/4 saloon, the Leyland Retriever received a new engine and repaint, the Dennis lorry was treated to an engine overhaul and a then very young Paul Porter completed the restoration of a 'Cyclemaster'. A number of the 'LeTall Collection' vehicles also received attention, enabling them to return to the road for the first time in quite a number of years; these included an Austin 10, the Austin 12, the Austin 18 and the Leyland TD7 bus plus the Bristol Lodekka. The cars required servicing plus attention to the fuel system (the 12) and a new exhaust (the 18). The TD7 was treated to an overhaul by Ford & Slater plus a full external repaint, whilst the Lodekka received attention to its back axle, this last item being kindly financed by long-standing member Andy Colley. The culmination of this hard work was a record turnout of vehicles for the finale of the 1982 rally season in September at Norfolk Park in Sheffield. Vehicles attending were a Morris 8 Series E, an Austin 10, the Austin 18, the Morris Commercial lorry, the Lodekka, the Bristol K5G, the ex-Jersey Leyland Lion LT1 and the AEC Regal – a truly remarkable feat which has perhaps not been surpassed to this day.

If this were not enough, in 1982 further work was carried out on the premises under a Manpower Services Commission/Community Enterprise Agency project. Replacement window frames were fitted in the museum extension, a toilet block was constructed and the annexe/canteen was completely renovated. Improvements were also made to the rear storage building with the building of a new brick rear wall and a new hardcore floor. Several vehicles were parked 'offsite' next door, courtesy of Tony Green, whilst this work was completed. Members' efforts on Society vehicles were also supplemented by the Community Enterprise workers, who assisted with ongoing restoration work on the Leyland Badger.

During the early/mid-1980s the Society was also fortunate to have some very interesting and unique vehicles on loan to supplement the museum display; a Jackson car owned by Jackson Shipley Ltd, plus a Bean 15 cwt truck and a Morris E Series car owned by Mr Reg Brearley.

With the advent of the Society's Silver Jubilee in 1984 a number of challenging issues occupied the minds of the then Committee. Yet further attention to the premises was necessary in the shape of the roof of the rear storage building, which had deteriorated to a dangerous state – this was tackled by members later that year with the fitting of new roof trusses plus a new roof. The possibility of the Society becoming incorporated as a limited company was also considered for the first time and subsequently discounted. A decision was also reluctantly taken to stop having a stand at the Lincolnshire Show, a local event that had been supported every year since 1966, due to the high site fees (though we did subsequently attend this event for several more years from 1986 onwards). On a more positive note, the Society enjoyed quite a coup with the annual Open Day that year, attracting Lynda Chalker, the then Under Secretary of State at the Department of Transport, as the Official Opener. Just a month earlier another leading celebrity of the day, Lord Denning, had ridden on the Leyland Lion PLSC1 from the Judge's Lodgings in Castle Square to the Greyfriars Museum in Free School Lane to attend the 'Lincoln Comes of Age' exhibition.

The November/December 1983 Society Newsletter featured an article by Steve Milner entitled *'The End for No. 5'*, lamenting on the perilous state of the Society's very first vehicle. As the history books show, this plea did not fall on deaf ears. Some twelve months later the items and rubbish that had accumulated within its body shell were removed and a lodger in the form of a field mouse was evicted. Then, and as reported on BBC TV's Look North, the Leyland Lion LT1 single-deck bus, with a locally-built Applewhite body new to the City in 1929, was moved to Lincoln City Council's Stamp End depot for restoration by council works staff, a sum of £25,000 being set aside for the project. The restoration of this veteran was completed just in time for the 1986 London to Brighton Run in May where, to the delight of City Councillors and Society members, it was awarded first prize in its class. This was a truly remarkable achievement, given that the body had been in a state of virtual collapse when the vehicle departed for Stamp End. No drawings or other details were available and the body had been reconstructed from patterns and photographs. A brief period of further active duty ensued on City Tours with the Transport Department before No. 5 took up residence once again at Whisby Road.

Towards the end of 1985 the Society was very pleased to accept one of the youngest vehicles ever offered to us – a 1970 Co-op Morris Minor van. At the time these were still fairly commonplace, but the decision to take one of the true motoring classics at such a tender age has since been vindicated over the years.

During the mid- to late- 'eighties work progressed on a number of 'new' restoration projects, alongside the regular love and attention required to keep some of the longer established vehicles in running order. Pete Francis and David Howe had gone to work on their SS Jaguar saloon and Neil Scully was putting a lot of effort into 'FDO', his ex-Kime's AEC Regent double-deck bus, plus his Riley car. Finally, Don Teesdale and his nephew Edwin Cattle were doing sterling work on their Bedford

The Co-op Morris 1000 van.
ANDY HIDES

The Bedford MLD flatbed lorry following restoration.
DON TEESDALE

VEHICLE PROFILE – VL 1263 (Lincoln No. 5)

A 1929 Leyland Lion LT1 with an Applewhite 32-seat body

An LT1 Lion, one of four that Lincoln Corporation took delivery of with bodywork by a local coachbuilder, Applewhite of St Rumbold Street. They had experimental concrete floors when new, which led to them being christened 'the Leyland Fireproofs' by staff.   No. 5 remained in passenger service until 1949, after which it gained a new lease of life as a snowplough. In 1954 No. 5 was sold to Sid Twell of Ingham, in whose yard it languished until being donated to the Society in 1959. Dry-stored for the next twenty five years, the body had deteriorated to a very poor state by the time it was selected as an apprentice training scheme project by Lincoln City Council in 1985/6. Restored to pristine condition, No. 5 saw further active service with Lincoln City Transport on City Tours duties before returning to the care of the Society.

Left: As acquired in 1959, stored in the yard of Young's Bodyworks.
COURTESY OF LINCOLNSHIRE ECHO

Below left: Seen here about to depart for the Council's Stamp End depot.
LVVS COLLECTION

Below right: Under restoration by Reg Cheetham and his team.
LVVS COLLECTION

Immaculate – a credit to all concerned.
STEVE MILNER

The idyllic setting for the 1986 Annual Rally in the grounds of Lincoln Castle, with the Cathedral clearly visible in the background.
PETER GREY

MLD flatbed lorry, which had been supplied new by Charles Warner Ltd to C Pratt & Son and had spent its entire working life making deliveries to the licensed trade in and around Lincoln. The Society's Leyland TD1 also had its engine stripped down and rebuilt, plus its seats retrimmed, whilst 'ONO', the Society's globetrotting tender vehicle, was treated to a repaint during this period. One setback suffered at this time was accident damage to the cab and nearside wing of the AEC Monarch, but in true Society tradition repairs were soon underway to get this tipper lorry back on the road in time for the 1988 London to Brighton run.

In the autumn of 1986 the Leyland Lion PLSC1 had to dust down its 'Equity' card at short notice and head off for deepest Wales to appear in an episode of the BBC TV series 'District Nurse' in the care of Pete Francis. Interestingly, in the following year, Pete's wife, Pam, became the first lady driver on the Society's insurance. Then in 1988, the Society gained truly international recognition with the recruitment of a member from Canberra, Australia, who owned a 1933 Humber Twelve.

1989 marked the Society's 30th anniversary, and to celebrate this milestone a social evening and disco was held at the Sincil Bank Community Centre in April, followed by a display of Society vehicles in the Castle Square later that month. The edge was rather unfortunately taken off these celebrations with the sad news of the deaths of two gentlemen to whom the Society owed a great deal. One was our founder member, Mr Vincent LeTall, and the other was Mr Herbert Jones, the former Lincoln Corporation Transport Department Manager and long-serving President of the Society.

As the Society entered the 1990s restoration work continued unabated. Further work was undertaken on the AEC Monarch's problematical engine and the

Badger also received considerable attention in an effort to get it back on the road after an absence of too many years. Attention was also given to another member of the LeTall collection, the Leyland Tiger TS7, which was treated to a mechanical overhaul and repaint. In 1990 Carl Langton acquired and set to work on a 1969 Daimler V8 saloon, whilst Pete Francis and David Howe continued with their endeavours to restore their SS Jaguar to 'concours' condition. Steve Milner was also making steady progress with his 1946 ex-Lincolnshire Bristol K6A double-deck bus, which had ended up in his care after passing through several owners since first being acquired for preservation in 1978.

The arrival of a new decade also prompted a rethink of Society events. By this time the Summer Rally had become a fixture at Lincoln Castle and was growing in popularity and success year-on-year. The annual Open Day in contrast was becoming something of a headache – development of the land surrounding the Museum had led to our usual rally site over the road disappearing. Ultimately, for 1991, the Committee decided upon a new format with the emphasis on encouraging the general public to come and have a look at 'what we are all about'. Gone were the days of a traditional rally season opener with upwards of 200 vehicles attending from around the region; there would in future only be limited space for visiting members' vehicles by arrangement, courtesy of one of our neighbours, Tony Green. Extra parking facilities were secured with the kind agreement of the Lincoln Co-op at their Moorland Centre off Tritton Road, linked by a regular free bus service to the Museum to cater for visitors, who were requested not to park in and

Three cars from The LeTall Collection on wedding duties.
PAM FRANCIS COLLECTION

Top left: LVVS vehicles seeking temporary refuge in premises kindly made available by Jackson Shipley Ltd whilst the building works were in progress.

Top right and lower left: Two views of the new exhibition hall during construction.

Lower right: The finished building about to be sampled by the Leyland Merryweather fire engine.
ALL: STEVE MILNER

Below: Vehicles from the collection mingling in their new surroundings.
LVVS COLLECTION

around Whisby Road. Sound familiar? The basic concept of our ever popular Easter and November Open Days as we know and love them today had been spawned!

The other major matter occupying Committee members' minds at this time was the state and layout of the ex-NAAFI Museum building. It was rather eloquently described in the Summer 1991 Society Newsletter in the following terms:

'It is of wooden construction and really doesn't lend itself to vehicle displays, due to the many pillars incorporated in the design. Besides that it is now old and getting quite saggy and grotty in places. Someone said it is a bit like a utility wartime Guy bus being purchased in 1966 when well-time expired, and still being used in the 'nineties!'

The Society's vehicle collection had recently been swelled by the bequeathing of the nine remaining vehicles in 'The LeTall Collection' on the death of Mr LeTall, and it was only too clear that urgent action was required if the positive progress made over the preceding 30 plus years was to be maintained. The Committee of the day accordingly decided that this building should be replaced by a new one with single-span construction, so that 'besides having a superb collection of vehicles we can have somewhere decent to show them off'. A separate building fund was duly launched, with accumulated Society funds of £30,000 being allocated towards the anticipated costs of around £150,000 to make this pipe-dream a reality.

During the summer of 1991 stardom once again beckoned for the Leyland Lion PLSC1 – this time for the BBC's 'You Rang M'Lud' TV series. Not to be outdone, fellow Lion No. 5 was taken by David Howe and Brian Bloomfield on a tour of Durham, Newcastle and York for the 'East of England Heritage Trail' in conjunction with the 1992 Milk Race, and in late 1993 this same vehicle travelled to Saddleworth Moor to appear in an episode of Granada TV's 'In Suspicious Circumstances'.

In the Summer 1993 Newsletter the Committee was pleased to advise the membership of the outstanding news that The Society was to benefit from a grant of £50,000 from North Kesteven District Council towards the cost of a new museum building. In no time at all the old former NAAFI building had been demolished and Beckside Construction went to work on erecting a steel portal framed replacement clad with plastic-coated steel sheeting. The 9,600 sq ft of accommodation incorporated such refinements as 20th century toilets, insulation, a concrete floor and halide lighting. By early November the work was complete, allowing for the official opening of the new exhibition hall building on Monday, 8th November at 1pm, with a party of NKDC Councillors as our special guests. Logistically, this project was perhaps the biggest exercise ever undertaken in the history of the Society, but, as usual, Society members rose to the challenge and the job was done. A large proportion of the vehicle collection was very generously housed by Jackson Shipley Ltd over the summer months whilst others were squirreled away at members' houses and at least one bus found its way into Lincolnshire Road

Car's St Marks Garage, where it could be observed mingling casually amongst its present day counterparts. The building programme and upheaval didn't mean that work on the vehicles ceased though; the ex-Co-op Morris 1000 van was checked over for an anniversary event that October whilst No. 5, the ex-Lincoln Lion, had a front brake service in readiness for the 'In Suspicious Circumstances' filming work mentioned previously, the lighting being provided by members' car headlights! During 1993 vehicles from the collection also attended events as far afield as Halifax and North Weald.

The opening of the new exhibition hall heralded a new chapter in the Society's growth and development, plus its establishment as a leading road transport museum in the East Midlands. Under the terms of the grant, the Museum's opening hours extended to Sundays throughout the year in future, plus from Monday to Friday during the summer months, necessitating the employment of two museum attendants. As a consequence of the new building being a dedicated display area, the restoration and servicing of vehicles would now have to be undertaken in what was presently the rear storage building, for which a further appeal for funds was made, to fully enclose it as a structure and convert it into a bespoke workshop with a water and a 240v and 3-phase electricity supply. One downside of the redevelopment was the loss of the canteen facilities. This was soon resolved by the adaptation of the BMMO 'SOS' single-decker for these duties and it has since attracted many favourable comments from visitors in this role. In the months after the official opening a number of finishing touches were made to our new surroundings; Specialist Heat Exchangers of North Hykeham very generously supplied a new purpose built gate for access to the rear yard and the appearance of the front of the premises was improved, aided by a further £5,000 grant from North Kesteven District Council.

After all the excitement and upheaval during 1993, 1994 was more of a 'back to basics' year. Three core members of the bus fleet received attention; the former Lincoln Guy was treated to a service and an exterior repaint, whilst the ex-Lincoln Leyland TD7 also received some mechanical attention and a partial interior repaint. If this were not enough, the ex-Lincolnshire Lodekka tootled off to the Road Car's Newark garage where it received a replacement front axle plus front and rear road springs. On its return to Whisby Road it was then also treated to a repaint. This work

proved to be very timely, given that in January 1995 this bus also received its 'Equity' card for an appearance in Channel Four's documentary series on 'Classic Trucks'. The most notable development of 1994 however was the completion by Pete Francis and David Howe of their painstaking restoration of the 1939 SS Jaguar to 'concours' condition. To see this very fine vehicle pass

the Society's present rally calendar and a very important fund raiser. In October 1995 this was followed by the first 'Special Events' day, which subsequently grew into the regular 'End of Season' Open Day; this one incorporated a photo shoot of preserved ex-Lincolnshire Road Car buses posing in front of the soon to be demolished St Marks bus station and garage.

its MOT that July and then take to the road the following month, a few days after its 55th birthday and almost 30 years after being taken off the road, was a wonderful sight for all those who had witnessed Pete and David's untiring hard work and patience over the years.

It was also during 1994 that the first of the Society's collection of cars from the 1960s and '70s arrived at the premises in the form of the 1966 Hillman Super Minx Estate and the 1969 Ford Capri 1600XL. These two were soon followed by a 1971 Triumph 1500 in early 1995. Not to be outdone, in 1995 the first underfloor engined bus to form part of the collection was purchased by Bob Brewer and Steve Milner. This was a 1960 ex-Lincolnshire Bristol MW single-deck bus in which a black lace bra and a pair of Y-fronts were discovered in the cupboard behind the driver's seat following collection. It is understood that the owner of neither item has yet to come forward, whilst the bus has meanwhile been restored, complete with authentic period graffiti.

For the 1993 AGM it had been decided that the Society would sample 'The Lawn', a former mental hospital which had recently been extensively renovated by the City Council and adapted for use as a leisure amenity. This in turn led to the Annual Rally being switched to this venue for several years from 1994 onwards. Another notable development with events at this time was the Society's acceptance of an invitation to put on a display of vehicles and run a bus service on the airfield at the RAF Waddington Air Show on the 1st and 2nd of July 1995 – this has since gone on to become an integral part of

A few weeks earlier the ex-Lincolnshire Leyland Tiger had also appeared before cameras of a less stationary kind, taking part in a BBC TV drama 'Over Here'. An active year of events was then rounded off with the appearance of the Austin 12 both on TV and in the press whilst opening the Lincoln Christmas market.

At the 1995 AGM the Chairman was pleased to report that the quite large debt outstanding as the Society had entered 1994 had been cleared by the year end. This had been achieved by the sale of many surplus spares plus several vehicles, including the unrestored Ford Model T and the part-restored Packard Hearse. It was with great sorrow that the Society learned of the deaths of two pivotal members as 1995 progressed, Arthur Groocock and then Pete Francis, both of whom had served as past Chairmen during their long and active associations with the LVVS.

During the latter part of 1995 the generosity of members and friends who had responded to the workshop appeal enabled a start to be made on that project, the first works being undertaken including the construction of an inspection/maintenance pit in the workshop building and the laying of road planings in the front car park, driveway and rear yard. This was followed in 1996 by the construction and fitting of a new door to the workshop pit bay. With an eye to further development being undertaken in the future a 'Building Extension and Improvement Fund' was launched in November that year.

In 1996 the first of what has subsequently been a procession of centenary anniversary events was held;

this one being to celebrate 100 years of Leyland Motors at Leyland in June. In anticipation, much attention was focussed early that year on the ex-Jersey Leyland Lion LT1, to get it ready for a trip to and period on display at the Greater Manchester Transport Museum, from which it would travel to participate in the Leyland Centenary event. The Society also held its own 'Leyland 100' event

Amberley Chalk Pits Museum in deepest Sussex for a gathering of surviving TD1s to mark the birth of the Leyland Titan some 70 years previously – a round trip of over 450 miles for a sprightly 68 year old upon which it was accompanied by the freshly repainted 36 year old ex-Lincoln Leyland PD2! On the vehicle restoration front 1997 marked the start of one major project and the

that Easter, during which five Society Leylands featured on the Park & Ride bus service operated to and from the Moorland Centre, courtesy of the Lincoln Co-op. These were both Leyland Lion LT1s, the TD1, the TS7 and the TD7. Work was also undertaken on the Leyland Badger, enabling it to gain its first MOT certificate for 27 years later that year, and take to the road alongside all the Society's other petrol-engined Leylands at the Members and Friends Day in November.

The anniversary theme continued into 1997 when the Leyland TD1 double-deck bus travelled down to the

recommencement of another. The former was the ex-Smiths Crisps Albion lorry and the latter the ex-United Bristol L5G single-deck bus with pre-war style Eastern Coach Works bodywork. 1997 also saw a number of new arrivals at the Museum; Don Teesdale's former Mayoral Daimler Limousine, Phil Rhodes' 1927 Humber 14/40 saloon and a 1964 Mobylette – a stable mate for the 1950 AJS motorcycle that had come our way the previous year.

Early in 1998 the Society's growing spares storage problem was resolved in an ingenious way, by the purchase of a redundant double-decker from a local operator, Kime's of Folkingham. Work on Society vehicles continued unabated with the Leyland Tiger receiving an interior rewire and refurbishment, whilst steady progress was also made on both the Albion lorry and the Bristol L5G bus. As ever, the Society was prepared to try out something new and in 1998 a bus service was run between Whisby Road and Burton

Don Teesdale alongside his former Mayoral Daimler Limousine.
DON TEESDALE COLLECTION

Facing page: Ex-Lincolnshire buses in front of the shortly to be demolished bus station and garage at St Marks in Lincoln.
STEVE MILNER

Above: The five Society Leyland buses dating from 1927 to 1930 lined up in the Museum yard.
PETER GREY

Road to support a 'Steam and Oil Day' put on by the Museum of Lincolnshire Life. This proved to be very successful in attracting additional visitors, with a total of 486 passengers being carried. Not surprisingly, it has since become an annual event. In 1998 the Society was also back on the anniversary theme; in May the Lodekka travelled to Bristol to attend a 90th birthday rally for Bristol Commercial Vehicles and the November Open Day featured a celebration of 70 years of Lincolnshire Road Car, with no less than seven of that Company's former vehicles running in service.

Another first for the LVVS in 1998 was to have one of our vehicles, the Leyland Titan TD1, measured up by EFE (Exclusive First Editions), a leading die-cast model maker, and in due course appearing by the thousand in miniature! In the autumn of that year two members of the vehicle collection, the Leyland Badger and the ex-Jersey Leyland Lion LT1, departed for Ireland for use in the making of the film 'Angela's Ashes' based on the best selling autobiography by Frank McCourt and starring Emily Watson and Robert Carlyle . . . plus a Lion and a Badger of course. To round off another memorable year the remaining half of the workshop floor was concreted over the Christmas period, meaning that all that was needed now was a new roof! 1998 was also the year in which a certain car was donated to the collection, an Austin Allegro, of which more will be said later.

In 1999 the Society celebrated its 40th birthday and curiously it was a rather quiet year in comparison with 1998. That is not to say that nothing happened, but rather there was an established pattern of very successful events and activities befitting a well-known and respected entity in vehicle preservation. Of note were the Leyland TD1's visit to Blackpool in May to celebrate 100 years of public transport in Bolton (to be with a former Bolton tramcar now restored and operating in that town in case you were wondering) and then in July the Museum suffered from major flooding, though fortunately no lasting damage was caused. Finally, in October the roof of the workshop building was replaced and finished just in time for the November Open Day. As far as the vehicle fleet was concerned 1999 was a milestone in one respect, it marked the start of the most comprehensive restoration ever undertaken on a Society car, the 1937 Ford V8 shooting brake. Finally, and with an eye to the New Millennium, 1999 marked the creation of the Society's website.

Due homage to the New Year and Millennium was marked by an evening meal and get together by LVVS members and their guests in February, and then it was on with business as usual. A coach shell was purchased from Lincolnshire Road Car for a nominal sum to provide

The Leyland TD1 at Blackpool alongside the privately restored and fully operational Bolton tramcar.
TONY STEVENSON

The Austin 7 Club visiting the Museum in July 2000.
JOHN CHILD

additional spares storage and at the Easter Open Day a new appeal fund was launched to raise £30,000 towards the cost of the Society's future development plans and help secure grant funding on a like-for-like basis. Utilising the concept that an elephant is best eaten one slice at a time, the elephant or 'ellie' fund was born, in which slices could be purchased at £2 a time. An unusual sight one summer Sunday morning that year was that of the Museum car park packed to capacity with Austin Sevens of all types and descriptions when we welcomed members of the Austin 7 Club on a visit. In October we had visitors of a different kind; a film crew from The Discovery Channel, who filmed Don Teesdale's Bedford lorry and the by now restored Albion lorry chassis for their 'Former Glory' series, which was shown early the following year. Work on not only the Albion, but also the Ford V8, progressed well during a year in which several of the Society's motorcycles also received welcome attention, courtesy of a father and son team. The commercial vehicle representation within the collection also grew in 2000 with the addition of two Morris vans owned by the Lincoln Co-operative Society.

In 2001 it was the turn of the Society's bus fleet to expand with the addition of a pair of relatively contemporary and local Bristols. In February an ex-Lincoln Bristol RE single-deck bus was kindly donated by Messrs Craig Tilsley, engine restoration specialists based in Staffordshire. Shortly after arrival at Whisby Road this bus was instrumental in securing an additional, albeit temporary, family membership for the LVVS – Feathers the Blackbird, who promptly took up residence and built a nest on the radiator! Though basically sound and complete, this vehicle is in need of liberal doses of tender loving care and copious quantities of cash, but hopefully one day...who knows? The second Bristol followed later in the year, having appeared at our Easter Open Day whilst still in active service. This was the RoadCar's last VR double-decker to remain in service, dating from 1980, and arrived in an all-over bright yellow livery reflecting its final role as a school bus.

During late 2001 and early 2002 several major steps forward were achieved in the long-term development of the Museum. The Society was very fortunate to be awarded a grant of £4,750 from the Heritage Lottery Fund under 'The Awards for All' scheme, to help with the costs of resurfacing the front yard, producing up to date publicity leaflets and the provision of brown direction signs to the Museum. In spring 2002 the Society's application for Museum Registration, a national 'standards assurance' scheme, key to securing further grant funding and on which an enormous amount of work was put in by the then Vice-Chairman Sandra Rhodes, was despatched for approval. The day after these developments and progress had been proudly announced at the 2002 AGM, the Society was saddened to learn of the death of John Marwood, an active member for 30 years who had served as Treasurer, Chairman and then Secretary during his time with the LVVS.

The ex-Lincoln Bristol RE being delivered to the Museum.
JOHN CHILD

Facing page: The LVVS stand and the Vulcan bomber at the 2001 RAF Waddington Air Show.
COURTESY OF THE RAF WADDINGTON PHOTOGRAPHIC SECTION

The ex-Lincolnshire VR still sporting the 'School Bus' livery in which it was acquired.
JOHN CHILD

As far as the vehicle collection was concerned, it was pleasing to see the AEC Monarch lorry back on the road in 2002 after yet further attention to its engine – this time a replacement cylinder head and radiator top tank had been fitted in an effort to make it behave when on the road. It made a welcome reappearance at the AEC90 Event at Newark in May, where it attracted much attention. Work on the Ford V8 was ongoing and it attended the RAF Waddington Air Show in a partly restored state the following month. Later in the year came news that the Society's application for provisional 'Registered Museum' status had been approved (with full registration being approved the following June) and that the LVVS had been awarded £4,250 by Lincolnshire County Council towards various vehicle restoration projects at the Museum – the Ford V8 shooting brake, the Bristol VR and the Leyland TD7 buses, the Albion lorry and the Austin 16 car all benefiting from these funds.

By the arrival of the 21st century serious consideration and debate was again taking place about the future legal status of the Society. The question of members' liability was becoming a serious issue and concern in a growing 'blame and claim' culture and culminated in an extraordinary general meeting being called in September 2002. At that meeting it was resolved that the Society would become a company limited by guarantee known as the Lincolnshire Vintage Vehicle Society Limited. This was duly incorporated on 13th December 2002 and the existing Society was subsequently wound up on the transfer of all the assets to the new entity.

What had been quite a memorable year in terms of achievement was rounded off on a pleasant and fitting note with the appearance of some members of our vehicle collection on both the big and small screen – several cars appeared in a film 'Anita & Me' released in November and in December one of the Co-op vans appeared on Channel 4's 'Battle Stations'. Finally, also in December, the preamble to a 'Bargain Hunt' programme was recorded at the Museum.

With the Easter 2003 Open Day the Society went back on the anniversary trail to celebrate 75 Years of Lincolnshire Road Car. A special commemorative programme was produced for the day and no less than nine out of the thirteen buses and coaches that took to the road on service were past or present members of the Road Car fleet, dating from 1935 to the present day and including our own Bristol VR bus, which had recently returned from the paint shops in the rather more discerning and respectable NBC leaf green and white livery in which it had been supplied new. With an eye to another birthday in 2004, 100 years of the City's own transport undertaking, much time and effort was expended during 2003 in ensuring the four restored examples from the City of Lincoln fleet were all prepared

Left: The AEC Monarch lorry at the AEC 90 Rally in 2002 with Society members Bryan Challand, Peter Parkinson, David Howe and Brian Bloomfield.
JOHN CHILD

Below: Celebrating Registration.
SANDRA RHODES

and ready to run in service on the day, aided by the RoadCar, who kindly repainted the ex-Lincoln TD7. Notwithstanding this, it was pleasing that remedial work was completed on the 1937 Austin 10 saloon to enable it to take to the road again after a ten year rest.

In the period since the new exhibition hall was opened the Society had acquired a steady stream of road transport 'furniture' and artefacts to complement the vehicle displays, including such items as a traditional GPO K6 phone box and an early City of Lincoln green street lamp. In May 2003 we were fortunate to add to this collection an original AA roadside call box, courtesy of the British Motor Industry Heritage Trust at Gaydon.

2004 saw another innovative event appear in the Society's rally calendar for the first time that March, 'The Discover Greater Lincoln Weekend'. The Society's willingness to work with other museums in the area and the local councils to promote tourism in and around

Lincoln led to the Society providing a free vintage bus service linking the various participating attractions, all of which offered free admission to the public. From modest beginnings this has since grown steadily year-on-year, with bus services being provided both within the principal tourist area in the City taking in the Cathedral and Castle, and a more rural service to Whisby Nature Park and Doddington Hall. A month later came the Easter Open Day, celebrating 100 years of Lincoln Corporation Transport and Lincoln City Transport. Over 500 visitors attended and 2,000 plus individual bus journeys were made on the day, for which another commemorative programme was produced. That July the Leyland PLSC1 bus was a star turn at the 'Leyland 120' event at Leyland, being transported there by low-loader, courtesy of Benton Brothers of Boston. In September this particularly busy year continued with a special event at Whisby Road to celebrate Museum Registration, at

which Society members and guests consumed liberal quantities of food and liquid refreshment and could sample a selection of vehicles that were giving rides.

Whereas in 2004 events had provided the most noteworthy news, in 2005 it was the turn of the vehicles. Over the 2004/5 winter the Leyland TD1 bus was treated to an overhaul of its brakes whilst the slightly younger Leyland TS7 had its engine stripped down and various component parts sent away for reconditioning. Attention was also given to the 1947 Austin 10 so that it could be out and about in Austin's centenary year – the first time it had been on the road since 1979! The most notable achievements though were the completion of two long-standing restoration projects that had been underway at the Museum for some years; one was the Society's 1937 Ford V8 Shooting Brake and the other Steve Milner's 1946 Bristol K6A double-deck bus. It was very gratifying to see both these splendid restorations of local vehicles

VEHICLE PROFILE - FW 9805

A 1937 Ford V8 shooting brake

This unusual vehicle has a 3.6-litre (30hp) V8 side valve engine, a 3-speed gearbox, cable brakes and a 6-volt electrical system. These cars were popular on large estates for shooting parties, and were regarded as good performers by 1930s standards, with a top speed of over 80mph. This example was presented to the Society by the Dowager Countess of Yarborough and has now taken to the road again after a lengthy absence following a comprehensive restoration.

Restoration in progress. *BOB BREWER*

The finished item – restored to its former glory.
ANDY HIDES

back on the road and attracting smiles and looks of amusement/disbelief from people on Lincoln's streets after an absence of over 35 years.

In late 2005 the Society's vehicle collection grew by the addition of two exhibits at opposite ends of the road transport spectrum, one a 1980 ex-Lincoln Bristol VR double-deck bus seating 86 and the other a butchers delivery bike from Brigg capable of transporting one, or two if you don't mind riding in the basket! Lastly, and by no means least, the Society was also pleased to accept from Lincolnshire Police two display engines made by apprentices at Longbridge.

Early 2006 saw the vehicle collection continue to grow in diversity and interest with the donation of an unusual 1953 Reliant goods tricycle by Simons Group Ltd, who had originally acquired the vehicle as a replica of the very first vehicle owned. By this time the engine rebuild of the Leyland Tiger TS7 had been completed, leaving only a poor starting problem to cure, and the Albion lorry

The Reliant van, pictured here in 'as acquired' condition.
LVVS COLLECTION

also now boasted a repanelled body. March 2006 also saw a unique event at the Museum; the launch of a book on 'Lincoln Corporation Transport 1904-1991' by long-standing member Cyril Cooke.

The continuing steady trickle of new additions to the collection had led to the exhibition hall and workshop accommodation at Whisby Road becoming increasingly cramped and to a degree hampering both the smooth operation of the Museum and vehicle restoration work. Being acutely aware of this, plus a desire to upgrade and improve the working environment at the premises, the Board became increasingly focussed on exploring ways in which additional space and facilities could be sourced. With this in mind, in April 2006 representatives of the Heritage Lottery Fund visited the Museum to discuss and give feedback on our future aspirations. The advice and guidance received has been most useful in helping the Board map out a future course for the Society, more about which later.

In September 2006 the Society was very sorry to hear of the death of a member since the early 1970s, a former school teacher, AEC fanatic and aluminium drink can recycler extraordinaire, Tony Peart. Out of regard for the LVVS and its achievements during his lifetime, Tony left us his two immaculate AEC double-deck buses plus his Doncaster residence, which was to be sold to provide funds for the housing and upkeep of his vehicles.

During the latter part of 2006 some useful progress was made on the never-ending queue of vehicles requiring attention. The Leyland Badger was partially rewired and a starter motor was fitted to enable it to take part in the End of Season Open Day, whilst the Morris 1000 van received an overhaul of its front suspension units. The rear springs and radiator of the Chevrolet LQ coach were removed and sent away for repair and the

Tony Peart's two immaculate Roe bodied AEC Regents.
JOHN A SENIOR

Leyland Tiger's fuel pump was returned from Scotland after overhaul . . . in a bus that had travelled down from the Scottish Vintage Bus Museum at Lathalmond to attend the November Open Day!

The steady progress that had been made in recent times on the Bristol L5G bus had also not gone unnoticed by the Transport Trust, who selected the project for a £750 award to assist with its completion. The Lincolnshire County Council Heritage Grants team also continued their staunch support of the Society with a sum of £1,500 towards the restoration of the Allegro. This support seemingly gave rise to 'Allegromania' in the media, with the vehicle and project featuring in the Lincolnshire Echo, BBC Look North, Radio 2, Radio 5 Live, Radio Lincolnshire, The Sun and the Daily Mirror! Whilst some of the press coverage was not overly complimentary to this vehicle, it did perhaps do justice to one of the Society's key objectives; to preserve examples of road transport history from every era of motoring for the enjoyment of future generations.

2007 also marked the centenary of the coachbuilder Plaxtons of Scarborough. Given that our little Badger has the oldest known Plaxton bus body in existence, in April it became the second vehicle to attend a rally from the Museum courtesy of a low-loader. The following month the AEC Monarch lorry, the Morris 1000 van and both Tony Peart's AEC Regent buses attended the 'Great North Road Transport Extravaganza' hosted by the AEC Society at the Newark & Notts Showground. It was believed to be the first time both Tony's Regents had attended a rally together, given he was in the habit of rallying one vehicle one year and the other the next.

As 2007 progressed the need to do something about the accommodation and facilities at Whisby Road became increasingly pressing. The arrival of Tony Peart's two buses, the Reliant tricycle previously mentioned, plus a 1966 Rover 2000 saloon in the preceding twelve months, has required the liberal use of member's 'little grey cells' and a shoe horn to fit them all in undercover. In August a number of Board Members met with North Kesteven District Council to discuss relocation possibilities as part of a proposed Regional Country Park Initiative. This was followed in October by an 'Ideas Meeting' to give members an opportunity to discuss requirements for a new museum should the Society relocate. Following this meeting several other options, including an extension

Steve Milner and Adrian Henson receive the Transport Trust Award from HRH Prince Michael of Kent for the restoration work on the Bristol L5G bus.
LVVS COLLECTION

Above, the vehicle responsible for 'Allegromania' in the local and national media, and below, the Rover 2000 saloon, both pictured here at the Museum.
BOTH: JOHN CHILD

on the existing site, have also been examined to ensure that whatever option is finally chosen will be the best for the future growth, development and sustainability of both the Museum and the collection. At the time of writing agreement has yet to be reached on the way ahead and

An overview of the 2007 Castle Rally from the walls of Lincoln Castle – from the opposite end to that on page 20.
MARIANNE BULLOCK

the Board remains in active discussion with several construction companies concerning the possible further development of the present site, and North Kesteven District Council over possible relocation to a larger site in the longer term. Whilst this debate has been in progress the Society has fortuitously received a substantial legacy from the estate of Mr Ken Pilkington, a former local lorry driver with a serious interest in transport, which will help us achieve our goals.

In the first part of 2008 two new exhibits arrived at the Museum, both of them true icons of the motoring of yesteryear. In 2007 Mr Ruddock finally took away the Austin Seven that had been on loan to us for 30 years and we were very pleased to replace this with another

UH 1773, the 1926 Ford Model TT truck.
ANDY HIDES

very fine example owned by Mrs Catherine Wilson, who had previously been a member, serving on the then Committee back in the 1960s. Then, at the Castle Rally in June, Society member Larry Riches presented the Society with a 1926 Ford Model TT truck, a gap that had long existed in the LVVS collection. In the autumn these were joined by a more youthful exhibit in the form of a 1991 Rover Maestro, which is in truly remarkable condition and was kindly donated to the Society by a Mr Piper of Newark.

At the other end of the spectrum one of the Society's very first vehicles, the Leyland Lion PLSC1, was treated to four new rear tyres at a cost in excess of £1,800, to enable it to attend a Leyland Society event at the National Tramway Museum, Crich, in July. A most enjoyable day out was had by all who attended, with this sprightly 81 year old romping to deepest Derbyshire and back in what seemed no time at all and without missing a beat. 2008 also saw the Leyland Tiger's reluctant starting problem finally cured, and the same team of engine doctors then went to work on the Leyland Merryweather fire appliance to get it back on the road. Finally, mention must also be made of the Reliant goods tricycle, which made its debut at the RAF Waddington Air Show following restoration.

2008 also saw a small band of volunteers, very ably led by Paul and Joyce Jefford, expend many hours revising and producing a set of six policies and plans covering various aspects of Society activities. Whilst these are in part a formalisation of practices and procedures that have evolved over the years, they have been produced in association with the Society's application for 'Accreditation' of our Museum by MLA (the Museums, Libraries & Archives Council). Accreditation is the next step on from Registration, which was obtained in 2003, and is key to the Society's continued growth and development in the 21st century. As we go to press the outcome of this application is eagerly awaited.

And so, as we approach the 50th anniversary of the Society, how much has been achieved in half a century? The Society has grown from nothing to a membership base of around 200, owns its own land upon which a purpose built museum has been erected and in which

in excess of 60 vehicles ranging from bicycles to buses and other exhibits are housed. The latest accounts show a solid and stable financial situation with healthy year-on-year surpluses and assets in excess of £1million. The events calendar is a stretching, varied and enjoyable schedule for our active members, with a range of events to suit every taste. The Annual Castle Rally, where the Castle grounds are packed to capacity with 200 or more cars, motorcycles and smaller commercials, and the End of Season Open Day, which in 2007 attracted around 1,000 visitors to Whisby Road, who made 2,900 passenger journeys on the 30 buses and coaches that were in service on the day (and for which the Society won the 'Best Event' award under the Lincolnshire Renaissance Heritage Awards Scheme), are but two examples. Then, there are the thousands of people transported to and from their cars at the RAF Waddington Air Show each year, courtesy of the Society's Park & Ride bus service. One would hope that, if Mr LeTall is looking on from above, he would give us a nod of appreciation for our achievements in his usual understated manner. But then, those of us who had the pleasure and indeed honour to be acquainted with the Society's visionary and founder member would know only too well, in his next breath he would be exalting us on to even greater achievements in the years to come.

It is fitting that the last word in this brief history should be one of thanks to the many, many individuals and institutions who have helped the Society over the years to attain the place it holds in the esteem of so many of our visitors, our colleagues in the museums sector, our fellow transport enthusiasts and others. We do not wish to omit even one of our benefactors from this sincere expression of thanks – so, paradoxically perhaps, we will name none.

Adrian Henson
LVVS Company Secretary
January 2009

The 1935 ex-Lincolnshire Leyland Tiger TS7 caught here in a quiet moment at a rally.
JOHN A SENIOR

Society members Peter and Margaret Parkinson pose alongside the car, now in the Society's care, that they courted in and used at their wedding in 1958.
COURTESY OF LINCOLNSHIRE ECHO

RESTORATION IN PROGRESS – FHN 833

A 1940 Bristol L5G with an ECW 35-seat body

Supplied new to United Automobile of Darlington, this bus spent its final working days from 1956 onwards with Greyhound of Sheffield, carrying workmen from the Lincoln area to power stations then under construction in the Trent Valley. It was purchased for preservation by the Society in 1962 and restoration commenced in 1970, but has proved to be problematical due to the intricate curved wooden body frame. Good progress has been made in recent years though, and it is hoped that this very rare vehicle will once again be seen on the streets of Lincoln in the not too distant future.

Looking tired and down at heel, the Bristol is seen here in service as a workmen's bus with Greyhound of Sheffield.
LVVS COLLECTION

Society members re-covering the Bristol L5G's roof with Calico.
LVVS COLLECTION

Captured here, having emerged briefly from the workshops to pose for the camera.
STEPHEN DODSWORTH

RESTORATION IN PROGRESS – FTL 138

A 1951 Albion HD55 6-wheel box van

The renovated chassis and partly finished cab are seen here at the RAF Waddington Air Show.

This vehicle was originally operated by Smiths Crisps as an open platform wagon, in their once familiar dark blue livery complete with gold leaf diamond trademark. The lorry utilises Albion's own 6-cylinder diesel engine and is one of two such vehicles acquired by the Society. The box van body it now carries has come from sister vehicle FTL 277. This has provided an invaluable and absolutely essential source of spare parts in the restoration of this vehicle, which is now at an advanced stage, as can be judged from the photograph alongside.

The present state of play, above centre, shows an impressive and attractive box van whilst the lower view shows the donor vehicle
ALL: JOHN CHILD

RESTORATION IN PROGRESS – AFY 376

A 1934 Austin 16 Berkeley saloon

The one member of 'The LeTall Collection' yet to take to the road, in the workshops awaiting attention.
JOHN CHILD

First registered in May 1934 at Southport by Jardines of Morecambe, it was licensed as a hackney carriage at an annual rate of £10.0s.0d. When broadcaster the late Wilfred Pickles was at Morecambe for a summer season, this car was used to transport him to and from his hotel in the Lake District. It was last licensed to the end of December 1961, and was subsequently acquired from Jardines by Mr LeTall in 1972, along with the very rare Chevrolet coach in the collection.

RESTORATION IN PROGRESS – SVL 185

A 1961 Austin Gipsy fire tender

This factory fire tender with a 2.2-litre petrol engine was owned by Ruston & Hornsby and used at its Waterside factory in the City. It was donated to the Society at the end of its working life and is currently being restored.

'Work in progress'.
ANDY HIDES

PART 2 –

A SELECTION OF ITEMS WHICH HAVE APPEARED IN PRINT OVER THE 50 YEARS

An Extract from 'Commentary from City and County' by the Gossiper – Lincolnshire Echo, Saturday, April 4th 1959
Reproduced with the kind permission of the Lincolnshire Echo

4. *Tel: Lincoln* 1160

THERE is a search on for an old Lincoln Corporation bus: if you know of one of the right vintage, there is honour in store for it. The searcher is Mr. Frederick Le Tall, of 137 Doddington-road, Lincoln, and the bus he is looking for is one of a fleet of Leyland Lions which the Corporation ran in the late 1920's. Mr. Le Tall is an old passenger vehicle enthusiast — as some people collect pictures and numbers of locomotives, he collects buses — and he is anxious to see the formation in Lincoln of a branch of the Vintage Passenger Vehicle Society. But first he wants that old Leyland Lion!

* * * * *

From his own records he knows that Lincoln Corporation bought 12 of them round about 1928: He even knows their registration numbers — VL 77, VL 300, VL 600, VL 601, VL 604, VL 658, VL 659, VL 660, CH 7905, CH 7907, CH 7908 and CH 7915. The last four were bought secondhand from the London Midland and Scottish Railway Company; their registration is Derby. Eventually, as they became worn out for normal service, they were all sold — but no one knows what became of them. The most likely thing, of course, is that after a possible further short tour of road duty, they were broken up for scrap.

* * * * *

But Mr. Le Tall hopes that perhaps someone who reads about his search may know something that will lead him to one.

BUS B-AND-B

He has actually found a Leyland Lion, but it was not one of Lincoln Corporation's. And what is more, thought it is permanently parked and used as a bed-and-breakfast place for long distance lorry drivers, its working parts are all present — and they work! With Mr. Herbert Jones, Lincoln Corporation Transport Manager, who is doing what he can to help Mr. Le Tall in his search, he went to see this 30-year-old bus at Torksey and they were both astonished to find that the engine still ran. But the owner needs it for his B-and-B business — though he will let Mr. Le Tall have the engine if he finds a body to put it in.

* * * * *

Mr. Le Tall has traced several other Leyland Lions. One, which had been in service in Jersey, is now owned by the makers, Leyland Motors Ltd., another, also from Jersey, belongs to the Vintage Passenger Vehicle Society, a third is still on duty in Jersey, where it is used for training bus drivers — and a fourth was last heard of in a scrap yard on the Dover road.

* * * *

If his search for a Lincoln Leyland Lion fails, Mr. Le Tall hopes that somewhere he may find one of the same vintage which was in service in some other locality. It is then his intention to have it painted in the Lincoln colours, put into running order and used by the local enthusiasts for outings to bus undertakings in the area. A local firm—Young's Bodyworks, Ltd.—have already offered to assist with the restoration of the body, and Mr. Le Tall hopes that other local firms might enter into the scheme with offers to deal with the rest of the vehicle. But first, he has to find That Bus—and, incidentally, a place to keep it in!

SATURDAY LINCOLNSH

COMMENTARY FROM

City and County

by THE GOSSIPER

LINCOLN WEATHER

Notes And—

The following are the readings (for the previous 24 hours) taken at Lincoln Corporation Climatological Station at 9 a.m. (G.M.T.) today.

	Temp. (F.)		Rainfall
Bar.	Max.	Min. G. Min.	Ins.
30.073	62	42	36 nil

Sunshine hours: 1.8

—Lighting Times

	p.m.	a.m.
Tonight	7.12	to 4.57
Tomorrow	7.14	to 4.55
Monday	7.15	to 4.53

Mr. F. V. Le Tall, of Lincoln, whose hobby is the collection of photographs and records of old buses, is anxious to find one of Lincoln Corporation's fleet of Leyland Lion singledeckers of 30 years ago. This is what they looked like: there were 12 of them. (See "The Gossiper").

WEDNESDAY   LINCOLNSHIRE ECHO   NOVEMBER 18, 1959

COMMENTARY FROM *City and County* by THE GOSSIPER

COLLECTION OF OLD BUSES

FROM Mr. F. V. LeTall, secretary of the Lincolnshire Vintage Vehicle Society, comes a report on the first six months' working of this unusual body, which was formed last April. Its original name was the Lincoln Vintage Vehicle Society, but, because of the interest aroused outside the city, its title was extended to embrace the county. The society possess four buses — two from Jersey, one from a scrap yard at Cammeringham, near Lincoln, and the other from Lincolnshire Road Car Company, Ltd. — and they have the offer of another but its purchase, from Jersey, is held up through lack of funds.

* * * *

The first acquisition was a 1929 Leyland single-decker which had formerly belonged to Lincoln Corporation: it has been completely dismantled prior to restoration to its original condition. Then came the two from Jersey, both Leylands, one made in 1927 and the other in 1930. They were recently shipped to the mainland and driven the 150 miles to Lincoln by members of the society without any trouble whatever — a tribute to the makers of the vehicles and to the people who had been responsible for their maintenance.

* * * *

The 1935 bus obtained from the Lincolnshire Road Car Company, Ltd., is not officially "vintage," but, says Mr. LeTall, it soon will be and they decided to acquire it while it was available.

THE ONLY ONE

The bus which is now on offer from Jersey Motor Transport Company Ltd. is one which the society are very anxious to add to their fleet. It is a Leyland high-bridge double decker — originally built for demonstration — and, as far as the society can ascertain, is the sole survivor of its particular type still in running order. Its cost, including shipping charges, will be £88 but at present the offer has had to be turned down because there is insufficient money in the kitty. Perhaps someone reading this and being interested in the activities of the society might like to help!

* * * *

Another pressing problem facing the society is finding covered accommodation for the vehicles to enable the members to work on them during evenings and weekends, the intention being to organise excursions in them next summer. The society are also hoping to licence their oldest vehicle in the near future and run it over all the Lincoln Corporation bus routes.

'FROM VISION TO REALITY'

John Child has been chatting with several founder and/or early LVVS members and here are some of their recollections.

Part 1 – The Birth of the Society
The words of a founder member, Dennis Hauton

I saw the article in the April 1959 Echo, rang up Vincent LeTall, and was invited to meet him in his High Street offices. Vincent showed me his extensive collection of photographs of local buses, and encouraged me to join a group of like-minded individuals to form the LVVS. Within a few weeks the first meeting took place at Vincent's offices, attended by Vincent LeTall, Sid Twell, Bryan Challand and myself, and we formed a Committee. By the third meeting a few weeks later Herbert Jones had joined and offered the Lincoln Corporation Transport's Board Room as a venue for future meetings. By that time Bill Heath had also joined, so the Committee comprised Vincent LeTall, Sid Twell, Bryan Challand, Herbert Jones, Bill Heath and myself. These were the founder members of the Society.

Part 2 – The Founder Members
Don Teesdale on Vincent LeTall
Don joined the Society on 27th May 1960 and still has his original membership card to prove it!

I had always been interested in vehicles, so I went along to 137 Doddington Road, knocked on the door and Vincent answered. I said, 'I am interested in the Vintage Vehicle Society'. He got hold of my coat and dragged

Vincent LeTall

me in – this was my first experience of Vincent – quite dramatic! Within a week I was the Chairman.

Vincent was a very unusual man in many ways. He focussed on old cars, old buses and his business. He was not 'a joiner' – he did not join the Rotarians, the Freemasons or any of the like, but he was devoted to his family – his wife and a daughter who survive him. His grandfather was Alderman Fred Higgs, a famous local character – he was the owner of the trams in Lincoln prior to selling out to the Corporation. Fred Higgs's daughter married Harry LeTall, who was Vincent's father. The LeTalls were a milling family based in Princess Street and all the LeTalls went into the business except Vincent. Fred Higgs had a chain of tobacconist shops in Lincolnshire, and Vincent took on that business.

Vincent was a man of habit to the point of obsession – he went to the same hotel in Scarborough for twenty nine years! He did everything according to a timetable. Twice a week he used to go round his shops and would expect the shop boy to be outside on the pavement to meet him at the precise time he was due to visit. Vincent was well known locally, and was able to converse with and influence important local people. He was a friend of both George Rock and Herbert Jones, one-time General Managers of Lincoln Corporation Transport. For a time every bus in Lincoln also carried an advert for his business, hence the use of the garage for initially housing LVVS vehicles was perhaps assured. He was a very nice and courteous man, but at the same time could be very impatient – he had two offices, one in High Street and the other at the Stonebow and walked up the High Street from one to the other on the road rather than the pavement so people would not get in his way.

Then there were his recruiting methods; he would stop important people in the street and say, 'Have you got £5?' Most knew Vincent to be quite wealthy and were surprised to be greeted in this way. They would give him £5 and he would then say, 'You are now a member of the Lincolnshire Vintage Vehicle Society'. Some members so recruited stayed with the Society for a long while, the most well known being John Scott, a local jeweller who remained a member until he died a few years ago. The Town Clerk used to walk on the other side of the road when he saw him coming!

He was also not averse to recruiting national celebrities of the time. He got the Bachelors to join the Society by going to the stage door of the Savoy cinema. One of them had had some publicity about an interest in old cars and that was enough for Vincent. He caught them on the way out, and they became honorary members. He did the same thing with Rupert Davies, who acted the part of Maigret, the well known TV detective in the 1960s. He came to open a local steam engine rally and was interested in vintage cars, so a party of us took him up to the Barracks in No. 1 with Bill Heath driving. There are also recollections of Acker Bilk meeting up with the Society on one occasion.

Vincent was very particular in his approach to everyday cars – he didn't keep them long and had a succession of Austins. He once bought a new Austin in two shades of green, a Westminster which was a six-cylinder version of the Cambridge. On delivery from Young's garage he listed 200 faults. It went back to the works on a trailer – he would not have it driven. And they put it right – but it took so long that in the meantime he had bought another car. So when it came back he put it in his garage and there it stopped with only 1,600 miles on the clock.

When I took over from Herbert Jones as Chairman, the Committee comprised Dennis Hauton, Brian Challand, Mike Dobson, Vincent LeTall (Secretary), Bill Heath and Herbert Jones. Herbert Jones was President and did not want to continue as Chairman – this is why I got the job so quickly. I continued as Chairman until 1974 and Vincent was the hard working Secretary for most of that period. He sat there, did as instructed and didn't dominate meetings, but fired pointers from time to time for us to consider – like, 'I have found a bit of land down Whisby Road and it's £750'. I remember responding, 'Very good but we haven't got £750', to which he replied, 'I am the Secretary and you are the Chairman – go and find it.' He was an ideas man and when Margaret Thatcher became Prime Minister, Mike Gallagher suggested that she should be invited to be the Official Opener at an Open Day'. Vincent duly wrote to the PM referring to her Lincolnshire origins and had a letter back declining but instructing the Minister of Transport to come instead – and she did.

Failing health finally took its toll and led to Vincent having to relinquish the role of Secretary and become a passive but keen onlooker of Society activities in the years leading up to his death in 1989.

> **Bryan Challand and Bill Heath**
> **Talk about other Founder Members**

Sid Twell

Sid Twell was one of life's real characters, always flamboyant and jovial, preferring a muffler to a tie. Highly intelligent and a true entrepreneur, Sid was not a fan of committee meetings, but was a very generous supporter of the Society over the years. Sid was well known and highly respected throughout the bus industry as a dealer in second-hand vehicles and spares. As a hobby he owned a race horse. Sid died in 1981.

Bryan Challand

Bryan Challand started his working life at Worthington and Simpson's, pump manufacturers at Balderton, and was then called up for National Service. In 1948 he went into the family garage business, working mainly on his favourite make of commercial vehicles – the AEC. Bryan was involved in the collection of the two ex-Jersey Lions from London docks all those years ago and has remained a member to this day, serving alongside Don Teesdale and David Hibbs as Society Trustees from 1993 until the Society became a limited company in 2002.

Dennis Hauton

Dennis Hauton was an avid bus enthusiast when at school. He started work at Smith Clayton Forge as a draughtsman, and worked for Hudson's of Horncastle as a clippie on Saturdays. Once he became time-served in 1962 he left the forge and went to work for Hudson's full time, serving as a manager for a while. In January 1968 he left Lincoln and went to work for Appleby's, for whom he still drives occasionally. Dennis was responsible for the first tours to the Arctic Circle, which proved very successful.

Herbert Jones

Herbert Jones came from a coal mining family, but his father wished him to have an office job, so Herbert trained as an accountant. He subsequently enjoyed a long and successful career in bus management, coming to Lincoln after being General Manager at Leigh, Greater Manchester. Herbert finally retired from the local transport undertaking in 1970 and continued to serve the Society as President for many years prior to his death in 1989.

Bill Heath

Bill Heath was the Electrical Department Manager of Warner's in Mill Road and went on the road selling 'Exide' batteries for that company in 1960, calling on Bryan Challand amongst others! In 1973 he purchased Greens Health Foods and relocated the business from the Cornhill to Vincent LeTall's former High Street premises in 1984. Bill finally sold this business in 2004 and has once again become an active member, helping out on Open Days.

Herbert Jones

The LeTall Collection Buses

Above left: TE 8318 – A 1929 Chevrolet LQ with Spicer 14-seat dual-door coach bodywork. Pictured here on display in the Museum.
JOHN A SENIOR

Above: FW 5698 – A 1935 Leyland Tiger TS7 with a 1949 Burlingham 35-seat body. Seen here awaiting its next service run at an 'Open Day'.
LVVS COLLECTION

Facing page

Upper: BFE 419 – A 1940 Leyland Titan TD7 with a Roe 56-seat body, now restored and in service at the April 1999 'Open Day', accompanied by fellow ex- Lincoln bus No. 23.
STEVE MILNER

Lower: LFW 326 – A 1955 Bristol Lodekka LD6B with ECW 58-seat bodywork. Waiting for passengers at the Moorland Centre on an Open Day.
ADRIAN HENSON

The ex-Lincoln Leyland Titan TD7 on the move from the rear of Mr LeTall's house in Doddington Road to the Society's Whisby Road premises.
COURTESY OF LINCOLNSHIRE ECHO

**TL 48 – A 1928 Austin Heavy 12/4 Clifton tourer. First
registered in Kesteven, it had four owners before being
acquired by Mr LeTall in 1961.**
LVVS COLLECTION

JV 4936 - A 1936 Austin 18 saloon. First registered and used by the local Austin dealer in Grimsby, it was acquired by Mr LeTall in 1969 and now sees regular service as a 'wedding limousine'.
LVVS COLLECTION

VL 8960 - A 1937 Austin 10 saloon. Supplied new to the LeTall family milling business, this car was a 21st birthday present to Vincent, and was used on his honeymoon plus subsequent family trips to Scarborough.
LVVS COLLECTION

CVL 212 - A 1947 Austin 10 GS1 deluxe model saloon. A relatively rare survivor of the post-war Austin 10; this example was owned by a local teacher prior to acquisition by Mr LeTall.
LVVS COLLECTION

'Vintage Viewpoint: – The Lincoln Rally'
by PJ Marshall (Publicity Officer, VPVS)
An extract from Buses Illustrated – October 1960

Reproduced with the kind permission of 'Buses' & Ian Allan Publishing Ltd

Vintage Viewpoint:—

The Lincoln Rally

By P. J. Marshall
(*Publicity Officer, V.P.V.S.*)

ON Saturday 19th July, I witnessed an event which can only be described as the most spectacular vintage vehicle rally enthusiasts are likely to see for a long time. It was held at R.A.F. Skelleythorpe, about three miles from Lincoln City, and was partly sponsored by the Lincoln Vintage Vehicle Society, mainly to arouse local interest in old-time vehicles, buses in particular. The programme included a grand opening by film star and actress Carol Leslie, followed by Go-Kart racing and a parade of horse-drawn vehicles, sideshows and a good deal of support from the Army, which included roasting an ox.

Approximately 14,000 people attended, paying admission fees of 2s. 6d. for adults and 1s. 3d. for children, arriving by car and public transport. During most of the afternoon the road from the airfield was one solid jam, with Lincoln City Transport and the Lincolnshire Road Car Co. operating a joint service from the city; in fact the scene from the rally enclosure could only be compared with a big race meeting.

Three buses were entered by members of the Lincoln Vintage Vehicle Society, a 1927 Leyland PLSC Lion (KW 474) ex-Jersey Motor Transport, a 1931 Leyland LT2 Lion (TF 818) also ex-Jersey, and a 1935 Leyland Tiger ex-Lincolnshire Road Car Co. All three vehicles looked very smart after having all the finer details polished.

Although very little restoration had at the time been carried out on the two later vehicles, the PLSC Lion showed that an outstanding amount of hard and tedious work had been carried out on it, although even in this case much remains to be done. Eventually, this vehicle is to be restored as a replica of the City's one and only PLSC Lion of that type, No. 4.

The Leyland Lion PLSC owned by the members of the Lincolnshire Vintage Vehicle Society first entered service in 1927 with Blyth & Berwick of Bradford and, together with their business, was taken over by the West Yorkshire Road Car Co. in 1928.

350

'Buying Our Land'
Extract from a document loaned by Don Teesdale
'Con-Rod', 40th Anniversary Issue – July 1999

Resolutions to be submitted to the General Committee of the Society on Thursday, 2nd May 1963, relating to the purchase of land on Whisby Road, Doddington.

Mr Day reported to the Meeting on the matter of the purchase of three-quarters of an acre of land fronting Whisby Road at Doddington. The price of the land was £750 and this money had been kindly loaned by six individuals as follows: -

Mr Frederick Vincent LeTall		£200
Mr Patrick John Lynch		£100
Mr William Edward Heath		£ 75
Mr John Dobson		£200
Mr Sidney Twell		£100
Mr Percy Wilfred Taylor		£ 75
	total	**£750**

The purchase of the land was then about to be completed and on completion it would be vested in Mr FV LeTall, Mr PJ Lynch, Mr WE Heath and Mr J Dobson, who would then hold as Trustees upon trust for themselves and Mr S Twell and Mr PW Taylor in shares proportionate to the amounts each had respectively contributed. At the same time as the completion of the purchase of the land, a Trust Deed would be executed and completed to properly put into effect the Trust.

Mr Day explained to the Meeting that the land, together with any buildings erected thereon of a permanent nature, would thereafter belong to and be owned by the four Trustees in trust for the six contributors until such time as the Society had repaid to the contributors the moneys contributed by them.

The terms of the agreement to contribute the money by the contributors was that the money was contributed for a period of four years from the date of completion of the purchase of the land, and that the Society would pay to each contributor interest in the meantime at a maximum rate of 6% or 1% above current Bank Rate (whichever was the greater). The interests of the contributors were protected by the fact that they could resell the land, together with any buildings thereon, after the end of the four years if the Society were then unable to pay back the moneys due to the contributors should it then also be impossible for new contributors to be found. Mr Day pointed out that, in the event of the Society having adequate funds with which to repay the contributors, the moneys which they had contributed, the Society should then be incorporated as a Company and thereupon acquire a proper legal status in its own right. The newly formed Company could then take a conveyance of the land in its own name.

'The Sobraon Barracks Depot'
by Cyril Cooke
LVVS Newsletter – Jan / Feb 1985

One evening in June 1965 I set out from my home near Burton Road to discover the LVVS.

I had been told by Mr LeTall, the Secretary at that time, to go along to the depot amongst the Sobraon Barracks any Monday night. Once there I was to make myself known to a Mr Padgham, the Depot Manager. So here I was, a young lad of fifteen, walking along Burton Road that I knew so well as it had been my paper round the year before. When I reached Breedon Drive I saw the old Ministry of Defence signpost with the three wooden arrows on it. One of these had been painted and stencilled LVVS; no doubt unofficially one dark night by some unscrupulous member keeping an eye out for the local 'bobby'!

Making my way along the drive I then had to find the building that was the Vintage Vehicle depot. There were a lot of buildings in the barracks at that time and I chose to look at the one on the left, just over the field at the end of Breedon Drive.

Outside, seated in a large Packard motor car was a gentleman to whom I asked – 'Excuse me; I'm looking for a Mr Padgham.' The reply was a little blunt, 'I'm him'. After introducing myself he took me inside the depot and told me I could have a look round on my own, that we were all friends here at the depot and that I too was welcome. I was introduced to a few of the members as the Captain. I thanked him, whereupon he left me to look around. As for the nickname, well I had never throughout my school life been called the Captain. Maybe I would get to like it, after all my name was Cooke.

As I began my tour, my first thoughts were as if I had just discovered a gold mine. The building was packed with old vehicles, including buses. This was the prime reason I was anxious to become a member. I was obsessed with old buses and longed to get involved with these enormous giants of the road. Here I could do just that – once I had paid my membership fee – and then I would be in my element.

There were nine single-decker buses in the depot and many cars bumper-to-bumper amongst them. There was also a horse drawn hearse, an old gypsy caravan and a tower wagon.

I looked at every vehicle in turn. To do this at the far end of the depot meant I had to climb over some of the vehicles, but I wasn't deterred as I wished to see them all. I remember three vehicles were in progressive stages of restoration. These were a Riley car owned by George Murray, the horse drawn hearse being beautifully hand painted and lined out by Fred Martin and the Leyland

Badger single-deck bus, being worked on by various members. The interior of the bus was being refitted by WR Davidson, better known as Rennie.

Seeing the work done inside the Badger bus aroused my enthusiasm and so it was that I made my mind up there and then that I would like to renovate a bus. One of the buses was in desperate need of renovation, in fact it needed rebuilding. This was the 1929 ex-Lincoln Corporation Leyland Lion No. 5.

Other vehicles that came to my mind housed in that depot nearly twenty years ago were a Rolls Royce saloon owned by John Fox; a Ford V8 station wagon and Singer Junior and Essex cars. In addition, there was a Ford Model T bus, Gash's Bedford bus, Leyland Lions Nos. 1 and 202, a BMMO SOS bus, an ex-United Bristol bus, an ex-Lincolnshire Leyland Tiger single-decker and a few more cars I am unable to put a name to.

Quite a collection!

Two views of the ex-Jersey Lions pictured outside the Sobraon Barracks.
LVVS COLLECTION

On my second visit to the depot, I was set to work with four other young lads by Bill Padgham, the depot manager, to wash down buses Nos. 1 and 202. These were being prepared for exhibition at the Lincolnshire Showground. I was told that this was the first occasion they had been brought out of the depot for many months. Judging by the amount of dust and pigeon droppings on the roofs, this was quite true. After giving the buses a good hosing down (and ourselves), we set to with scrubbing brushes on the roofs and wheels. A great deal of care was needed on the steeply contoured wooden roofs as we couldn't reach it all from ladders.

A great deal of elbow grease was applied and therefore sometime between eight and eight thirty we took a well earned break in the canteen. We all had a cup of Mike Gallagher's famous LVVS coffee. Made with tinned milk, it had a very distinctive taste and was very enjoyable with a packet of crisps or a Mars bar. Then it was back to the buses for a while longer. We finished our wash downs and made arrangements to meet up the following Monday evening to clean up the interior saloons of the two buses.

That evening we did just that. We cleaned, talked, and had our coffee and crisps. The two buses were then inspected by Bill Padgham and pronounced ready for the show.

As autumn came and went, and the nights became colder, attendance fell slightly on Monday evenings. None the less, mundane jobs were doled out by Bill to us younger members. We grumbled and protested and were told that if we didn't like being given the mundane duties, for example washing and scrubbing out buses, sorting piston rings and the like, then we should get down to some serious restoration work.

There appeared to be no shortage of vehicles waiting to be 'adopted'. My weakness was for double-deck buses, and as yet the Society did not own one, but was negotiating with Leyland Motors to receive a 1929 Titan. On one occasion I was confronted by our Bill, who had heard I liked woodwork, to have a go at the derelict Leyland Lion No. 5. After an unpleasant exchange of words I agreed to get stuck in on the double-decker whenever it arrived, rather than attempt No. 5.

For the next few weeks I left off going to the depot until one night in November. When I entered by the main door I looked straight away for the double-decker. To my delight it had arrived. I heard a shout, 'Hey, your bus is here.' I walked over to it wondering what I had let myself in for. She certainly was an old bus alright, the first I had seen of its kind, apart from in books. The top deck front was shaped like an upright piano. Inside, I saw that it was a lowbridge double-decker with a sunken side gangway.

It quickly became obvious to me that this was a rare find, for this was a Leyland Titan TD1. Not many of these buses were thought still to be in existence. This one had escaped the breakers yard, somehow. I had a good look over it and my first thoughts were that this vehicle would need a lot of hard work and hundreds of pounds to put it right.

Bill came over to talk to me and asked what I thought of it. I told him it would be a big task and it appeared to be worse than I expected. He replied, 'I thought you could do it, thought you liked double-deckers and were good at woodwork.' That did it. I wouldn't give in to defeat to this man, I thought, so I said I would work on the bus.

One week later and back at the depot, inside the double-decker, I wandered over my plans. Clearly the first thing to do would be to remove all the seats. This would provide working room to remove the interior wall panelling so that I could have a look at the condition of the body framework. The lower deck nearside wall was bulging outward and this suggested broken or rotten window pillars.

I carried out this work over the next few Monday evenings. Quite a few folk came to see the bus and have a chat. One of them was Steven Milner, then twelve years old and dead keen on buses. They all wanted to know how much work was involved. A look at the exposed frame gave them some idea of the scale of the operation, as did the falling roof and the sagging lower deck ceiling.

Throughout the winter Monday evenings of 1966 I carefully removed the windows and exterior panels. Now fully exposed for the first time in many years was the framework of our TD1; a crumbling mess of rotten timber.

News reached us that we would shortly have to leave the Barracks because the Corporation were going to develop the site for housing. All work on vehicles was halted and volunteers sought to dismantle a large wooden building at Dunkirk Road (inside the Barracks). Much of the demolition was done by a contractor in the week whilst the volunteers did much of the lorry loading on a Sunday morning. This arrangement worked well and enabled the contractor to make good progress on re-erection of the building at our museum site at Whisby Road.

The building was ready for occupation in June 1966 but by no means was it complete. Work carried on long after the move. The mammoth task of moving all the vehicles and equipment took place one weekend in June. Many of the vehicles were non-runners and had to be towed. The 1935 BMMO SOS ex-Trent bus was a stalwart, moving many loads throughout that weekend.

A task of this nature has to be well organised and without any doubt, would have been a shambles had we not had our depot manager, Bill Padgham, in sole charge of everything. Like it or not, he was the driving force behind the whole venture and credit to him. It was here that he acquired his nickname the Hos-Man because every time manpower was needed to push a non-runner, Bill would shout, 'heave and again, heave', like a horse man driving his horses on. No one ever addressed Bill with that name, but what I do know is that it was all light-hearted fun and I am sure he knew that.

'The Great Escape'
by Bill Dixon
LVVS Newsletter – Sept / Oct 1984

This article originally appeared in the December 1967 Newsletter and was reprinted in 1984 with a foreword from Bill Dixon, the then Newsletter Editor.

Foreword

The first name to appear in the Registration Book was the Secretary of State, Home Office, London, SW1, due to the appliance belonging to the NFS until 1948.

Under registration particulars were -

Registration Mark:	GLW 419
Description of Vehicle:	Turntable Escape
Chassis Type:	TD7 No. 307135
Make:	Merryweather

Also stamped in the book is the following -

No licence issued. Vehicle exempt in accordance with regulations made under the Emergency Powers (Defence) Act 1939.

The second entry to appear in the book under 1st change is that of Haylett; Edward George, Fire Station, Longdales Road, Lincoln, with the date: 11th April 1948.

The Great Escape

In June 1941, Lincoln City Fire Brigade took delivery of a new Leyland appliance, which was fitted with a Merryweather turntable ladder. Even at that time, there was no covered accommodation for the crew, and the appliance therefore had the appearance of an earlier model.

In 1966 an ERF fire engine, fitted with a Snorkel escape, was purchased to replace the Leyland. The change was prompted not by any defect or wear and tear on the Leyland, but by the necessity for the Fire Brigade to keep abreast of technical advances which assisted them in their commendable work.

After 25 years of faithful service, the Leyland had become something of a favourite at the Fire Station and the Chief Fire Officer, his officers and men, did not cherish the idea of the vehicle being broken up for scrap. The City Council added their support that scrapping

GLW 419 *en route* **to the Fire Brigade's new South Park Fire Station in 1964.**
LVVS COLLECTION

52

would be an ignominious end for a faithful servant and the idea that the vehicle should be put in the care of our Society for preservation was readily accepted.

The fact that fire engines are traditionally kept in the most perfect mechanical order and are always kept polished to a mirror finish, is now an English custom. The machine in question was certainly no exception to this rule and the Society was therefore proud to accept custody of the vehicle.

Thus it was that on November 4th, a ceremony was held at the Fire Station, South Park Avenue, Lincoln, to officially present the fire engine to the Society. Senior Society officers arrived at the Fire Station in Messrs Bartons' 1912 Daimler char-a-banc, whilst the Mayor of Lincoln, the Lady Mayoress, plus the Sheriff and his lady, were transported in the Ruston car.

An Open Day was being held to mark the occasion and after a display which featured both the old and the new machines together, the handover ceremony commenced. Our new Vice-President, Mr JW Stonehouse, took charge of the proceedings in his capacity as Chief Fire Officer. The Mayor made a most entertaining speech in handing over the vehicle on behalf of the City of Lincoln, and our President, Mr H Jones, was also on top form when he spoke to accept the vehicle on behalf of the Society.

Afterwards Mr Stonehouse made public a secret wish of the Mayor to drive the fire engine, and it also came to light that the Sheriff wished to accompany him, in order that he might ring the bell. After onlookers had been warned to stand well clear the Mayor took to the wheel and proved himself to be well up to the task. The Sheriff was also seen to be a most expert bell ringer.

The weather was not very kind to us, but this did not deter a large number of members from attending the ceremony, nor did it deter those who had agreed to take part in the parade from the South Common to the Fire Station. The line up included Mr Watson's 1930 Standard, Mr Tyler's 1934 Leyland Fire Engine, Miss Bowyer's 1933 Austin 7, Mr Rhodes's 1927 Humber, Mr West's 1928 Standard, Mr Moody's 1930 Bentley, Mr Padgham's 1935 Packard and the Society's 1930 Singer.

All present were invited to tea and biscuits by the Fire Brigade, and we were then able to inspect the Fire Station plus all the Brigade's vehicles. We must offer our sincere thanks to Mr JW Stonehouse and his staff for making the afternoon such a success.

GLW 419 pictured again, now in the Society's care and parked over the road from the Museum at the May 1988 'Open Day', and with the 1927 Dennis lorry for company. *PETER GREY*

'London to Brighton 1968'
by the late Peter Francis
LVVS Newsletter – January 1996

I had been a member of the LVVS for only a matter of weeks when plans were formulated for the 1968 London to Brighton run for commercial vehicles at the beginning of May the following year. The intention was to take four vehicles to the start at Battersea Park, these being the 1927 Leyland Lion, the 1930 Leyland Badger, the 1935 BMMO SOS and the 1942 Leyland Merryweather fire engine. For this we required twelve drivers. I still can't work out whether I was being honoured to be offered a drive or if I was just making up the numbers.

My experience of driving large vehicles was limited to the Ruston car and my father's Humber Hawk, neither being exactly gargantuan, so a driving lesson cum test was organised on the nearby and disused Skellingthorpe aerodrome. For this lesson we used the SOS. Anyone who is not used to driving old commercial vehicles will immediately be surprised by the throttle pedal being, not on the right, but in the centre of the brake and the clutch, and the fact that synchromesh was a thing of the future. However, after some appalling gear changes, I managed to reach top gear and was tearing down the main runway at what felt like 90 mph (actually about 25), when I started to approach the twiddly bits at the end. At this point I received the second surprise; the brakes were definitely in the lucky class, lucky they slowed you down at all, never mind pulled you up.

So it was that after a ten minute drive I became an experienced commercial vehicle driver, free to explore the Queen's highway at 30 mph.

Because I held the exalted position of committee member, I was placed in charge of one of the vehicles, the Badger, my assistants being Tony Wall, Cyril Weeks and a third person who I can't remember. Was it Paul?

Before I go any further I should explain that the Badger is a rather unusual vehicle, being a normal control goods chassis with a Plaxton bus body. The gear lever is therefore directly into the top of the box and not into a change speed box as is usual with a forward control bus. Should you match the road speed and engine revs precisely, the gears will engage without a murmur. Should you mismatch by just a few RPM, there will be an almighty crash, but the gear will engage. Should you be more than a few RPM out, forget it. You will break your wrist before the gear engages, and once you have missed the gear, the only solution for the novice is to stop, engage second gear and move off again. What I am really trying to say is, the gearbox is a PIG.

So we left Lincoln at 8am on a foggy Saturday morning, destination Battersea Park. Cyril took the first stint and was most definitely in the professional class of driver. Slotting the gears in with two fingers on the gear lever as you or I would in a Fiesta, instead of grit your teeth and go for it with all your might, we three amateurs began to

The Badger pictured below in the museum ...
JOHN CHILD

... and seen on the facing page repainted red and white for use in the filming of 'Angela's Ashes'.
STEVE MILNER

think that a fault with the gearbox had been miraculously cured and we would have no more trouble.

After about two hours Cyril handed over to me. Right! Select second gear and move off. After about fifty yards, dip the clutch, into neutral, release the clutch, pause, dip the clutch again and go for third gear. GRAUNCH. Funny, the fault seems to have returned. Stop. Select second gear and start again. After about two miles I managed to get into top gear. Now the secret is to read the road ahead very carefully so I stay in top, because if you think it was difficult going up the box, wait until you try to change down. The easiest way is to stop at the roundabout or foot of the hill, engage second and start again. Driving this way, it's an awful long way to London. Eventually Cyril perfected a solution. As I explained, the bus is normal control, so he would get the bus rolling along in top gear, set it on hand throttle, stand up and the next driver would slide in behind the wheel. In this way we reached Battersea Park and repeated the antics to get us to Brighton on the Sunday.

After a very enjoyable day spent looking round the other participants on the Run, we left Brighton about 5pm

for the journey back to Lincoln via London. Cyril took first drive as usual and then asked me to take over. 'OK', I said, 'as long as you take over again before London'. This was agreed and off we set. Little did I know that I had been set up, as Cyril went to sit on the back seat. As we approached the southern outskirts of London I shouted, 'traffic's getting thick Cyril'. 'OK', he replied, 'just a bit further and I'll take over'. After another two to three miles I shouted to Cyril and received the same response. We repeated these exchanges several more times until the heavy traffic forced me to concentrate fully on the gear change, the width of the bus, the length, the lack of brakes, the gear change….. When he did eventually relieve me, we were just north of Hendon heading for the A1.

I was tired, I was sweaty and I think I had lost half a stone, but by God I could change gear!

Postscript: This article was submitted by Pete to the Newsletter Editor on the eve of going to Germany (to work) for the last time before his untimely death in 1995 and is reproduced by kind permission of his widow, Pam.

In the Chair – Mr Teesdale.
Present - Messrs Walsh, Marwood, Flear, Groocock, Milner, Gallagher, Garton, Baumber, Francis – later Mr Charman. Mrs Flear, Mrs Francis – later Mrs Charman.
Apologies – Mr Bonsall and Mr Cox

Item 3; Proposed Recall of £1,000 Loan

a) The loan for £1,000 at 8% had at some time been increased to 9% and now repayment was being requested by 2nd September 1973. Another loan at 10% could be made available.

b) This action was not brought about by increased interest rates but through death; the money was required for the estate.

c) Mr Bonsall suggested by letter that we should not take out another long term loan but sell some vehicles unlikely to be restored.

d) The following possibilities seemed worthy of discussion;
  i) New long term loan.
  ii) New short term or bridging loan to gain time to think or raise money.
  iii) Multiple loan.
  iv) Apply for gift from Lincolnshire Association.
  v) Sell some assets.
  vi) Appeal to people and associations in town.

e) A save as you earn scheme would eventually pay off the loan. An advance subscription scheme could be put towards paying off the loan.

f) The outstanding money owed by the Society was; Land - £500, Loan - £1,000, other creditors approximately £80; a total of £1,580 to £1,620.

g) A proposition by Mr Milner, seconded by Mr Francis and passed unanimously was that we do not take out another long term loan.

h) A proposition by Mrs Charman, seconded by Mr Francis and passed unanimously was that we pay back £200, reducing the amount outstanding to £800.

i) Proposed by Mr Charman, seconded by Mrs Flear and passed unanimously that we apply to the Lincolnshire Association for a gift of £1,000. Mr Teesdale to motivate the claim.

j) It was agreed that we must have an £800 loan to clear the existing loan, and as the Treasurer would be away on business, Mr Teesdale would negotiate a loan on our behalf.

k) The multiple loan was attractive but it was decided as impractical because time did not permit all members to be notified.

l) It was decided that action would be taken only when a unanimous decision had been obtained.

m) The possibility of the sale of the following vehicles was discussed; Ford T, Essex black, Essex blue, Toastrack, No. 5, ADC, Vauxhall, Bristol bus, Citroen half-track, Morris Commercial, Horse drawn hearse.

After discussion it was proposed;

  i) By Mr Gallagher, seconded by Mr Flear and passed unanimously to obtain best offer for the ADC.
  ii) By Mrs Flear, seconded by Mr Milner and passed unanimously to obtain best offer for the Vauxhall. (Mr LeTall to be informed)
  iii) On the horse drawn hearse it was agreed to defer a decision to offer it to the Lincolnshire Association until Mr Charman had negotiated with Mr C Groombridge regarding the possibility of it becoming a money earner on outside contract loan.

n) It was proposed by Mr Gallagher, seconded by Mr Francis and passed unanimously that on Saturday 27th and Sunday 28th October 1973 a spares sale be held at the Depot, Whisby Road, Lincoln. It was agreed that other trade stands be invited and that the two cars be offered for sale during this weekend. Members to be told of the sale.

This item has been included to demonstrate that it has not been all 'plain sailing' over the last 50 years, and that some difficult situations have had to be faced up to, and dealt with, from time to time.

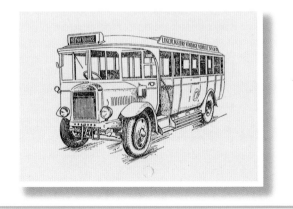

LINCOLNSHIRE
VINTAGE VEHICLE SOCIETY

Souvenir Ticket

6d. single

WOULD **YOU** LIKE TO JOIN

FULL DETAILS ON REQUEST

FOUNDED APRIL, 1959

'Cathedral Rally'
by Steve Milner
LVVS Newsletter – Sept / Oct 1980

It was heard that a special order had been put in for fine weather on the 13th July over a forty mile radius of Lincoln Cathedral. Whether that was true or not, the Society was certainly lucky in having one of the few Sundays of late when it was fine all day for its annual rally, which was held in front of the Cathedral for the second year running.

Our organiser, Arthur Groocock, had managed to gather together for the day a very interesting and varied collection of 44 vehicles; comprised of 11 commercials, 17 cars and 16 motor cycles, and there is no doubt that the west front of the Cathedral provided a magnificent setting for such a display.

By the time I arrived at about 12.30, most of the vehicles except for a few motor cycles were in position, with the ladder on the fire engine extended up to a modest 70 feet. Throughout the afternoon there was a steady flow of visitors and it was pleasing to see the interest being shown in the vehicles. It was said that at one time the three wise monkeys were seen sitting on the low stone wall for a while, but I think someone was being a little rude. One thing for sure though, one voice was heard above all others, and that belonged to our official programme seller. Well done Bert! No one can say that they were unaware that programmes were on sale.

Throughout all this, our two judges for the day, Gilbert Blades – a Lincoln Solicitor, and Leonard Marsh – Principal of Bishop Grosseteste College, ably assisted by Pete Francis and David Howe, were busily trying to find the winners, which could not have been an easy task in view of the very high standard of the vehicles on show. At about 4pm Leonard Marsh told me that they had reached their decisions and said quietly that they would creep away before the assassinations began. He need not have worried, they had done an excellent job.

At 5pm the Dean of Lincoln kindly presented the trophies to the winners, who were : -

Class 'A' – Motor Cars - The Sass Plate.

Mr Shaw of Scampton for his 1930 Austin 16/6 saloon.

Class 'B' – Motor Cycles – The Chummy Trophy.

Monty Mortimer of Tealby for his 1924 Sunbeam Light Solo 500cc.

Class 'C' – Commercial Vehicles – The LVVS Cup.

Colin Garton of Nettleham for his 1938 AEC Monarch lorry and trailer

Thanks to all concerned for a very pleasant afternoon.

The view from above the Rally shows how well the display fitted in with its impressive surroundings.

Following an official visit to the Museum by twelve members of the County Council in March, an approach was made to the Society to provide transport for the press and official party for the *Lincoln Comes of Age Exhibition*.

On April 11th our 1927 Leyland Lion, driven by Peter Francis, collected the press party from St Mark's Station. Arthur Groocock accompanied them and they were given a tour of uphill Lincoln before being deposited at the Greyfriars Museum in Free School Lane.

The Official Opening was on Friday, April 13th; again the Leyland Lion was driven by Peter Francis, this time accompanied by Margaret Henderson to look after our important passengers. Lord and Lady Denning were collected from the Judge's Lodgings in Castle Square and were accompanied by officials from the *Lincoln Comes of Age Exhibition*.

Lord Denning took a particular interest in the history of No. 1 plus the activities of the LVVS. Lady Denning said that her father owned the first car to be registered in London, and she had an accident whilst driving it (without permission), ending up in a ditch.

By coincidence the route chosen to the Greyfriars Museum was a very nostalgic journey for Lord Denning. His grandfather had a shop at 77 Bailgate, he passed the Racecourse where he used to play whilst on holiday in Lincoln as a child, and he pointed out the house in The Avenue where his grandfather used to live.

The Official Party was met at the Broadgate entrance to the Museum by the Mayor of Lincoln and the exhibition organisers, plus quite an array of photographers.

Our work now over, the bus and its crew returned to the depot, with considerable pride and thanks to all involved for a job well done.

At the August Committee Meeting my attention was drawn to the canteen notice board by the offer of a four day trip in Steve Milner's AEC Regal single-deck bus to attend the above rally. I quite fancied the idea of a weekend away with the lads, so during the drive home I plucked up the courage to ask my beloved (the wife) for a long weekend pass. This, to my surprise, was obtained with reasonable ease and without too much to pay in the way of reparations.

As ever, with an eye to the easy life, I had persuaded Steve that it would be best if the intrepid party negotiated the rural back lanes of deepest Leicestershire to come and collect me from my house. The thing I had not bargained for when they arrived, was being promptly placed in the driving seat with the instruction, 'now get us through Leicester and onto the Fosse Way'. We accordingly set off from Hall Orchard Lane, Frisby on the Wreake (next time we'll move to somewhere with a shorter name) at 8.15am on Friday, 30th August to begin our weekend of adventure.

This day proved to be one of the few fine, dry and warm days of the summer and yours truly settled down to thoroughly enjoy himself at the wheel of this majestic AEC. I eventually alighted from the cab some three hours later on reaching Burford, this being the first of many occasions during the weekend that certain members of the crew exhibited an aversion to pass public houses encountered on our travels without sampling at least one glass of their ale.

We arrived in Bournemouth mid-afternoon, our hotel being found with little difficulty as it had been stayed in the previous year. Unfortunately it had changed hands since then and was all rather forgettable, save the lasting impression the room I shared with Neil had on my poor head. Although the hotel was nearly empty we were given top floor rooms, the ceiling of ours being no more than 5ft from the ground. Needless to say, at the end of two days I had developed quite a convincing Quasimodo impression.

Around teatime we caught a 'Yellow Bus' into the town centre for a bite to eat followed by a leisurely stroll along the seafront. I lost count of the number of hostelries that were visited on the return journey, but readers may rest assured that 'falling down water' was consumed in some quantity.

Saturday morning started off dry and bright, so after some discussion it was agreed that we would visit the Bournemouth Passenger Transport Association collection and then head for Corfe Castle. The former was achieved with relative ease but the latter was an altogether different story. The Regal developed fuel supply problems and with the weather taking a turn for the worse, an umbrella proved to be an essential part of the tool kit. We never did reach the Castle; rather we limped back to the hotel where a proper repair was made with the kind assistance of the local National Express depot.

That evening Steve, Neil and I decided to have a ride on one of Bournemouth's open top buses. A word to the wise – riding on one of these is about as warm as riding a motorbike. After being swiftly transformed into three brass monkeys, readers will quite understand why the return journey was made in the lower saloon.

On Sunday morning everyone managed breakfast and then we made our way to Ringwood for the start of the rally. The vehicles assembled in Sainsbury's car park and in due course set off for Salisbury. There a refreshment stop was made at (yes, you've guessed it) another Sainsbury's. Of course, when we arrived in Bath we knew that our objective was to find that Company's premises in the town. (NB: I did consider calling this article 'A Tale of Three Sainsbury's') Actually, that company's car park in Bath is very interesting in that it is an adapted former railway station.

About a dozen buses, forty commercials and a handful of cars had arrived by mid-afternoon, which together made a very spectacular display of the transport of yesteryear. It was about this time that Steve and I decided to add a little culture to the weekend by taking afternoon tea at Bath's world famous Pump Rooms. After a spot of Darjeeling and a bun we returned briefly to the rally and then set off to find the excellent 'Strathavon' guest house.

Sunday evening was spent visiting various Bath publicans and on Monday morning we explored more of this most ancient city. By lunchtime it was decided to embark on our long journey home. A refreshment stop was made at Cheltenham Coach Station, which the Regal doubtless visited in service. Near Coventry yours truly climbed into the cab for another enjoyable stint as duty driver, notwithstanding the heavy rain providing a steady supply of cold running water inside the cab (sorry Steve!).

I arrived back home at around 6.30pm to be greeted by both wife and cat, both of whom I was assured had missed me. I, for my part, had had a most enjoyable four days and would like to thank all my travelling companions, and in particular Steve, for making this little adventure possible.

Steve Milner's former Enterprise Passenger Services AEC Regal at Poole Harbour.
STEVE MILNER

'Going the Long (Wrong?) Way Round'
by Betty Allen
LVVS Newsletter – August 1992

After lengthy planning and preparation Ken and I set off on 1st May 1992 in our 1935 Morris 10/4 to drive round the coastline of Great Britain.

Day 1; We went from Lincoln to Grimsby, over the Humber Bridge, picked up the A1033 and started the coastal route going up the east side of England. Our first night was spent at Redcar but the first day had not been problem free. There was a sudden loud bang – Ken thought it sounded like the cylinder head but it turned out to be a shattered plug. Luckily we had a spare and were soon on our way again.

Day 2; Dunbar was reached but the journey involved driving through the Tyne Tunnel where we had to use dipped headlights. One of our lights had come loose and was shining on the wall instead of in front. We were worried should it come loose and fall off, but it held until we could stop safely and tighten it.

Day 3; To Fraserburgh, running into very wet weather. Ken serviced the car before we set off again but it was wet and muddy, so not an easy task.

Day 4; To Dingwall, Ross-shire. A very nice drive with lovely scenery and no mechanical faults.

Day 5; To Bettyhill. It was really windy, entailing us moving the position of the tent for fear it would blow it and us away. We had crossed the John o' Groats landmark today and though it was cold, Ken having to drive in coat, cap and gloves (he did wear trousers, don't panic!), we were thoroughly enjoying the challenge. Unfortunately we drove over an unmarked ramp and the jolt loosened the wiring under the dashboard, so it was catching.

Day 6; To Kinlochewe. A lovely drive spoiled by such awful weather. We camped on a site run by the National Conservancy Council, which is free to anyone for up to three nights, the first time we'd ever found a free site in all our years of camping. What a night though, rain like you've never seen or heard – no chance of sleep, just a continual roar. I shone the torch out in the pitch dark because I was convinced we were in the middle of a flood. All that was visible was stair-rods of rain and slugs eating the paper label of the drinking chocolate jar, ugh!!

Day 7; To Oban. The weather was just awful; clothes wet, tent wet, car wet, everything wet! Rain had started to leak in through the roof of the car and there was yet another loud bang, which was the plug which had shot out again, but this time it didn't break and was replaced.

Day 8; Took us to Ardgarten, where on arrival the sun

The Morris 10/4 car pictured here on its travels.
Photo: BETTY ALLEN

broke through. People said they hadn't seen the sun for six weeks and it didn't last for long. As soon as the tent was erected the heavens opened again. It even snowed and hailed. The speedometer broke on the old car!

Day 9; Took us to Ayr, where we actually saw some sunshine. This was a shorter journey to take a break and visit my cousins. Daffodils were still in bud and the leaves still not unfolded. Farmers were only just putting potatoes in the fields; such a change in seasons up North. We drove back to the campsite after dark and I was really impressed with the old Morris. Not often driven after dark; it looked so lovely and was running so well.

Day 10; Heading for Carlisle. Weather was much better and it was a nice run. We stopped off at Gretna Green (we have been married since 1960 – honestly!); it was very commercialised but we enjoyed a lovely pot of tea and lots of people were interested in the car. We had just gone three miles, just back into Cumbria, when something really did go wrong. Ken thought it sounded like the big end. Nothing for it but to contact National Breakdown; what a blessing we'd taken that precaution! Within fifty minutes help was at hand via a young lad called Gary who took charge, loading the car and driving it plus Ken and I back home in three and a half hours. What does one do after such plans and dreams are shattered? One spends the night at home and sets off again the next day with the Montego, driving it to where we broke down and spending the night at Egremont on the eleventh day.

Day 12; Took us to Thurstaston and to the Wirral Country Park for the night. A wet and windy start, but better by lunchtime, still windy though!

Day 13; To Borth, camping on a very open and windy field amongst the sheep. Ken actually let me drive today. Using the old car Ken had to open and close the door for me, as it needs lifting whilst being closed. Now the fastener on the driver's side is broken so the position is reversed and I had to open the door for Ken.

Day 14; To Tenby. I drove to Fishguard. A lovely morning but a cloudy and windy afternoon. We went out for a nice meal in the evening and were the only occupants on the camp site again.

Day 15; To Gloucester to stay overnight with Ken's sister. The weather was gorgeous and we had to buy a new distributor cap for the Montego.

Days 16 & 17; At Damage Barton, near Ilfracombe. We were getting on faster in the modern car so we decided to stay to look around a bit more. This was the nicest place visited with lovely coastal walks, nice pubs and a bungalow for sale at Lee Bay, which was very tempting!

Day 18; Tregurrian, near Newquay, negotiating steep hills and hairpin bends. Maybe the old Morris would have struggled. It wasn't the same in the Montego; the fun and the challenge having gone.

Day 19; To Trelowarren, quite a thick sea mist and quite cold.

Days 20 & 21; to Torquay, and for a change, two nights in a hotel. The weather was just fabulous. Lots more traffic here.

Days 22 & 23; To Bournemouth and back to camping. The tent must have been placed on an ants nest, but luckily we had some spray in the car. The weather was fantastic again, unbelievably hot for May. The Montego's engine was playing up a bit!

Day 24; To Pevensey, the most crowded camp site visited, which was marked full shortly after our arrival. The Camping & Caravanning Club own the beach so it was not too crowded and although it is cobbles, it was very nice and it was sunny too.

Day 25; To stay with friends at Rainham, Kent. We stopped off at Broadstairs, a lovely little spot, the beach absolutely packed in the hot sunshine.

Day 26; Visited cousins at Westcliff-on-Sea and then stayed at Capel St. Andrew, near Orford.

Day 27; To East Runton. It was cooler and breezier with the odd shower; nice to be on the homeward stretch.

Day 28; We continued along the coast to Grimsby and then through the Wolds and home. We were surprised how busy the Lincolnshire coast was!

Twenty-two nights camping in one small pup tent with no air bed! The itinerary, summarised, had been as below.

    1 night at home
    1 night at Ken's sister's
    1 night with friends in Kent
    2 nights in a hotel

Expenses worked out at:

Petrol had cost	£296.69
Toll Bridge	£ 5.75
Camp fees	£ 69.70
Hotel	£ 48.00

Total number of miles covered 3,733 – the coastal route being 3,211.

Then the wondering – did we go the wrong way? If we'd gone clockwise would the car have been successful, or would it have broken down anyway?

The hard ground at the end of the journey felt just like a feather bed. Marks & Spencer sell the most delicious food, both fresh and in tins. Nice to be home, but a very enjoyable experience. Incidentally, in time a small tent becomes as much home as home itself, proving that home is where the heart is!

Ken Allen sadly passed away in March 2008. The car used for part of this little adventure is being kept by Betty, Ken's widow, in his memory.

'A New Home For Some Old Treasures'
by the late John Marwood
LVVS Newsletter – December 1993

It was an historic day for the Lincolnshire Vintage Vehicle Society on 8th November 1993. That day saw the opening of the new Transport Museum and was the culmination of many months of negotiations, planning, countless meetings and single-mindedness on the part of the Committee.

As is usual with an undertaking of this magnitude, there were quite a few unforeseen problems – not least bad weather which delayed the building work – and it called for a magnificent effort by all those involved to have everything ready on time.

However, when the 'red-letter day' dawned, we can confidently claim that all the hard work and effort had been justified. It was such a pleasure to see the new building 'spick and span' and at last some of the Society's vehicles displayed to their full advantage.

The opening ceremony began with an address by Margaret Henderson, on behalf of the Society, to over one hundred Society members, supporters and friends – old and new. After welcoming guests, Margaret outlined the Society's progress since its inauguration and described how the present day's achievements had been obtained through the co-operation of the Committee of quite a small Society with a supportive and enthusiastic local council and a most helpful, efficient and accommodating small local construction company. The local council being North Kesteven District Council and the builders Beckside Construction Company. Margaret felt that she had to mention two individuals who had put in such sterling work – namely Steve Milner, a Society committee member, and Clive Redshaw of North Kesteven District Council. She said that we are at the end of phase 1 and, although everyone could be pleased with what had been achieved so far, there is still much to be done and there is an exciting future ahead of us.

Margaret then asked Mr Tom Ball, Chairman of North Kesteven District Council, to perform the opening ceremony. Mr Ball opened his remarks with an anecdote about a much loved Alvis which he had once owned and went on to say that today's big step forward for

North Kesteven District Council Chairman Tom Ball and LVVS Chairman Margaret Henderson cut a celebration cake to mark the opening of the new Museum.
COURTESY OF LINCOLNSHIRE ECHO

A panoramic view of the Official Opening.
STEVE MILNER

the Society was the result of a successful partnership between the Lincolnshire Vintage Vehicle Society and North Kesteven District Council. He said he realised there was still some way to go but he was confident in the Society's ability to achieve its aims and could see the Council's continued support. Councillor Ball then officially opened the Museum by cutting the ceremonial ribbon and everyone then enjoyed a delicious buffet meal provided by North Kesteven District Council. A happy day was rounded off by the cutting of a magnificent cake baked and iced by Pam Francis.

A very happy day, which we hope is the first of many in the new Museum building.

Mrs LeTall seen in the family car used on their honeymoon.
JOHN CHILD

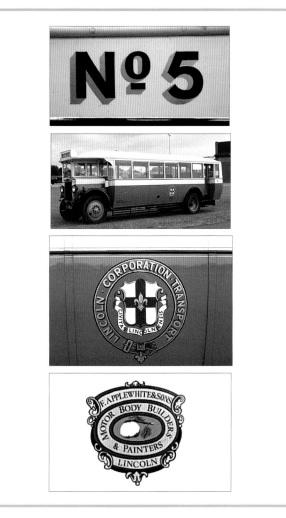

'Transformation at Lincoln' by Stephen Morris   Buses – April 1994

Reproduced with the with kind permission of Stephen Morris, 'Buses' and Ian Allan Publishing Ltd

PRESER

Last month's 'Preservation' looked at the future for the Cobham Bus Museum. It foresaw the future transformation of what was basically a vehicle store in a wartime building into an attractive museum, possibly with a little help from the local council.

A pipedream? Well hopefully not. And if the good people of Cobham ever doubt the possibility, they could do worse than pop up to Lincoln to see what the Lincolnshire Vintage Vehicle Society has achieved.

From shed to museum

The parallels between Lincoln and Cobham are very marked. Both have their origins in the late-1950s. Both were fortunate enough to have members with the foresight to buy suitable out-of-town sites. Both had very similar buildings; while the Lincoln folk didn't actually erect their edifice until 1966, it was, like the building at Cobham, a wartime shed. Like Cobham, Lincoln's building housed some real gems which were packed in like sardines in conditions which though secure and dry were scarcely salubrious.

Lincoln has already succeeded in enlisting support from the local authority, North Kesteven Borough Council — the premises are just outside the City of Lincoln itself. This has been in the form of a grant of £50,000 which has been combined with the group's own cash resources to allow the erection of a new £100,000 building.

The new building is now in place, and vehicles were moved in in November 1993. Although no great architectural gem, the new building — a typical modern steel-skinned industrial unit — makes a superb setting for the LVVS's very valuable collection of vehicles. It has a concrete floor, in which foundations have already been set for the later building of a small display area. It is all insulated, so in winter is not so bitterly cold as the old building could get. And it is spacious, allowing the collection to be shown to best advantage.

The next phase is to convert one of the remaining buildings behind the new museum into a workshop with a pit, lathe etc.

The vehicle collection

Not all the LVVS collection is buses. There is a fine collection of cars, and a few lorries as well. These certainly add to the appeal of the place, although further description of them is probably out of place here. Most of the bus collection is of local interest,

TRANSFORMATION AT LINCOLN

STEPHEN MORRIS has been looking at the Lincolnshire Vintage Vehicle Society's new museum in Lincoln. It sets a pattern which other societies could well emulate

Above:
The Lincolnshire Vintage Vehicle Society's new building. A fine-line-up of vehicles is headed by the Lancashire United Leyland Lion.

Above inset:
Prewar Leylands abound at Lincoln, including this ex-Lincolnshire Leyland Tiger TS7 of 1935, with a postwar Burlingham body.

although some are from further afield.

It is probably one of the best collections of prewar Leyland buses accessible to the public anywhere. There are no less than three Lions, two Titans, a TD1 and a TD7, a Badger and a Tiger TS7, the last admittedly with a postwar body.

The Lions are all in a fine state of restoration. Two are in Lincoln livery, although one, a PLSC, is really a West Yorkshire vehicle. The other, an LT1, is a pukka Lincoln vehicle with very rare Applewhite bodywork, built in 1929 to Leyland pattern, which was rebuilt by Lincoln City Transport before it was privatised. It is a magnificent restoration. The other, also an LT1, dating from 1930, is one of the famous vehicles from the early days of preservation, a Lancashire United vehicle with Roe bodywork whose rich red livery provides a strong contrast to the predominantly green collection.

The Badger is a very interesting vehicle, a small normal-control vehicle with Plaxton bodywork which was new to Bradford Corporation in 1930. It is largely intact, but needs a some tender loving care to bring it up to scratch. It is parked in a corner of the museum building in which there are several vehicles awaiting restoration. These genuinely look like part of the display rather than a handy place to store a load of wrecks; indeed an unrestored Vauxhall car has been placed in a rusting tin shed with straw on the floor to show how old vehicles are often discovered. A simple expedient yet remarkably effective. Also in the 'unrestored corner' are a three-axle Albion lorry from Smith's Crisps, an important local employer, and a delightful and now very rare Ford Model T with Baico extension, a one-time very common form of village bus, complete with what would now be called a demountable body for dual roles. It needs a lot of work but it is complete. New in 1922 it has bodywork by Fentiman, its Scunthorpe-area operator.

Another well-known vehicle from the early days of preservation, also from outside the Lincoln area, is the Bolton 1929 all-Leyland Titan TD1 with its open-staircase, lowbridge body. This, like the Lions, is now on full public view, and is also in a fine state of repair.

More Lancastrian vehicles in the collection are another gem, a 1929 Chevrolet LQ with Spicer 13-seat bodywork which originated in Morecambe, and, a direct successor of the Chevrolet, a classic Duple-bodied Bedford OB which came from a Warrington operator, in the days before Warrington miraculously swopped sides of the Mersey. And from further afield is a green RT, the newest bus on the display, which reached the museum in a deplorable state (begging the question as to whether London Transport's elaborate overhaul arrangements were all they were cracked up to be) but now looks very sound.

The rest of the bus display is purely local, comprising Lincoln's well-known all-Guy Arab with locally-made Ruston Hornsby air-cooled engine, unusual for a bus of its period in the amount of sound-proofing in the cab and under the bonnet, evidence that even by the standards of the 1950s it was a noisy beast! Apparently it is also very powerful, and drivers either loved it for its speed or hated it for the noise and heat in the cab — though the latter was of course an advantage in winter!

The Tiger TS7 is a 1935 Lincolnshire Road Car vehicle, with a 1949 Burlingham bus body which has recently had a repaint in Tilling green and cream. The Titan TD7 was built in 1940 to prewar specification and was new as

Lincoln 64, and sports a splendid Roe body which has almost a Gothic appearance. Finally the local independent sector is represented by FFU 860, a dual-purpose Willowbrook-bodied AEC Regal III from Enterprise, Scunthorpe.

There are plenty of other vehicles in store in various states of restoration, some familiar to rally-goers, some which we await eagerly, such as a prewar United Bristol L5G complete with prewar ECW body which looks quite far-gone, but restoration is proceeding apace and it is hoped it will see the light of day in restored state in the foreseeable future.

The LVVS certainly has a remarkable collection; one often wonders what has happened to some of the gems rescued in the early days of preservation, and yet here in Lincoln one can see a good number of them displayed to great advantage. The new museum is open on Sunday afternoons throughout the year, with no admission charge — but they'll happily take donations. It has been a long, slow achievement, but then bus preservation always is. It has been well worth it.

Above left:
In need of major restoration is this model T Ford village bus. Alongside is the unrestored Vauxhall car in 'as found' state.

Above:
Looking in fine fettle is one of the classic buses from the early days of bus preservation, former Bolton 54, an all-Leyland Titan TD1 with open-staircase lowbridge bodywork.

Left:
Detail from the fine former Lincoln Applewhite-bodied Leyland Lion.

'Restoration of a 1939 SS Jaguar 2.5-Litre Saloon'
by the late Peter Francis
LVVS Newsletter – April 1995

I first remember the car in the early 1970's standing in the Society's museum at Whisby Road. It was a typical old Jag – rotten from the windows downwards and completely worn out mechanically.

Three of our junior members, or youth club as we called them, had just purchased it for the princely sum of £25. The only point in its favour that I could see was its registration number – BUT 7. As an enthusiast of Riley and Porsche, it was unthinkable to consider a make of car popular with motor traders and bank robbers!

For some reason, these lads asked my advice on how to tackle the restoration, so I uttered the immortal words, 'first take the body off'. This was the last time I was consulted for many years. As any of you with pre-war cars will know, the only parts which hold the front half of the body to the back are the roof and the rocker panels, or sills as you would call them on a modern car. When the rocker panels have long since turned to iron oxide and deposited themselves on the Queen's Highway, there is not a lot of strength left in the body. With all eight body mountings having turned to the same red powder as the rocker panels, disconnecting the chassis from the body was not a major task. I can still see it as plainly as if it were happening today. Eight of us – two at each corner – lifting the body and folding in half in the middle so that each door aperture at the bottom became about a foot longer than original. My credibility took an instant nosedive. From this point on the majority of the chassis work was carried out by David Howe, one of the original trio, while I returned to work on my Rileys.

However, times change. I soon lost interest in the Riley marque and my second interest went the same way. A Porsche 911E found its way into my garage, but did not stay very long because it was a great disappointment. Maybe it was not a very good example, but when I was offered a straight swap for a V12 E-type, the decision was not very hard to make. This was my introduction to Jaguar motoring.

By this time two of the original owners had found other (female) interests, so David offered me a half share in the SS provided I sorted out the body. Like a fool, I said yes. Mechanically the car had progressed well. One of our members had cut out all the chassis rot around the body mounting points and welded in new metal. Some years previously the Society's spares department had cleared out the stores of an ex-Jaguar dealer in Lincolnshire and this provided a very useful source of mechanical spares. Other parts such as pistons, bearing shells, clutch and crownwheel pinions were obtained from other sources.

EVERYTHING was dismantled and reconditioned. At this time there were virtually no specialists in the field of vehicle restoration, so it required a great deal of thought and ingenuity in many instances.

Restoration well underway in 1989 with the body safely supported on planks before being relocated on its chassis.
PAM FRANCIS COLLECTION

The rebuilt engine was mounted on a wooden frame and run up before installation in the chassis to check that everything functioned correctly. We put off for as long as possible the refitting of the body, but eventually there was no excuse and it had to go back on the chassis – but exactly where? The only location points we had were a pair of reinforcing brackets on the base of the bulkhead which bolted through long slots in the chassis into captive nuts. We spent many weeks with a body jack, timber for packing and lengths of angle iron tack welded to various points to get the body in some sort of shape so that the doors would close properly.

The next problem was to make up the body mountings, but the remains of the originals were so vague that we hadn't a clue what they should look like. The chances of finding an all-steel SS at a rally were very remote and most of those we did see had been bodge repaired so badly that they didn't provide much of a reference. Progress over the next few years was very slow and would stop for many months at a time. Summer times were spent at rallies with the Society vehicles while winters were so cold in the old museum that any tools we picked up would stick to our hands; not a good recipe for enthusiasm.

Eventually we worked out what the body mountings should look like and proceeded to fabricate some new ones. This was in the days before DIY MIG welders

At a Castle Rally upon completion alongside Carl Langton's 1969 Daimler 2.5 litre V8 saloon.
PAM FRANCIS COLLECTION

became available, so everything had to be gas welded. The distortion produced by the gas welding had to be seen to be believed! We had one stroke of good fortune when we found a company with a set of drawings for the rocker panels. The panels they sent us were an almost perfect fit.

The turning point came, I think, in the mid-1980s. David and I were at the Beaulieu Autojumble in the constant search for parts and we bought a new set of tyres, a stainless steel exhaust and arranged to have the radiator rebuilt with an original type film core. Incidentally, the radiator was a replacement discovered at an earlier autojumble after the one belonging to the car had been stolen.

I think we had now reached the stage faced by many home restorers. The amount of money spent was quite considerable and the only way was forward. The car just HAD to be completed. Purchasing one of the new DIY MIG welders was a conscious effort to speed up the restoration, but the first one was returned faulty and the second one was sent back to the manufacturers so many times for repair that it would probably have been quicker to stick to gas welding. Eventually I bought a professional MIG welder and have had no trouble since.

By the late 1980s the body was again structurally sound so was taken off the chassis for repairs to the wheel arches, seat pans and scuttle. Before the restoration was finished we had had the body on and off so many times that we could drop it on and fit all the mounting bolts in about thirty minutes. While the body was off this time, we finished off the running gear. It was

indeed a red-letter day when one quiet Sunday morning we took the rolling chassis out for an illegal road test.

Once the body was complete we mounted it back on the chassis so that the rest of the panel work could be tackled. All four doors had the bottom 12ins cut off both the inner and outer panels, and new sections made up by hand. The boot lid received the same treatment, as well as having to replace the top edges. All four wings needed major surgery, but by far the worst job of all was the spare wheel door. The bottom 6ins was missing completely and although the top half of the outer was re-usable, the inner was so thin that it weighed a matter of ounces. The door shape, particularly the inner, is very complicated in order to clear the spare wheel, and the chances of finding another were as slim as being struck by lightning. The solution? Make another by hand. It took WEEKS. All four bonnet sections were very good, requiring only minimum welding.

We carried out the basic paint preparation ourselves but had the painting done professionally in Lincoln. The car was painted in the original olive green, a colour which bears a passing resemblance to the colour of army vehicles. Small wonder that the regulars at the Museum have nicknamed the SS 'Rommel's staff car'. Nevertheless the finish is superb and is as good as any we have seen.

The interior is typical Jaguar, all wood and leather. The wood was repaired, veneered and polished as necessary by a specialist in Spalding and the results speak for themselves. Although we would have liked to retain as much of the original interior as possible, partly due to cost, years of neglect and exposure had taken their toll. The company who refurbished the woodwork recommended a small organisation in Baston. Never have we seen such perfection. The cost was high but the finished result worth every penny.

Re-chroming was entrusted to a company in Birmingham as a result of a chance meeting at Beaulieu autojumble, and, apart from a few hiccups, has been first class. We finished the restoration in July 1994, the SS sailed through its MOT, and after some hassle arranging insurance cover it was taxed in August, a few days after its 55th birthday and almost 30 years after being taken off the road. The end result has far exceeded our expectations. For a 1939 car, it is very advanced in its drivability which is more like a car from the 1950s.

Would we do it again? When we think of the problems, the cold nights, the expense, the time it took – absolutely no way. The problem is, memory can be very short. We have just started the restoration of a 1956 Jaguar Mk V11M. Trouble is, it's a typical old Jag, rotten from the windows downwards and completely worn out mechanically!

The boot lid opens to reveal a well-equipped toolbox.
PAM FRANCIS COLLECTION

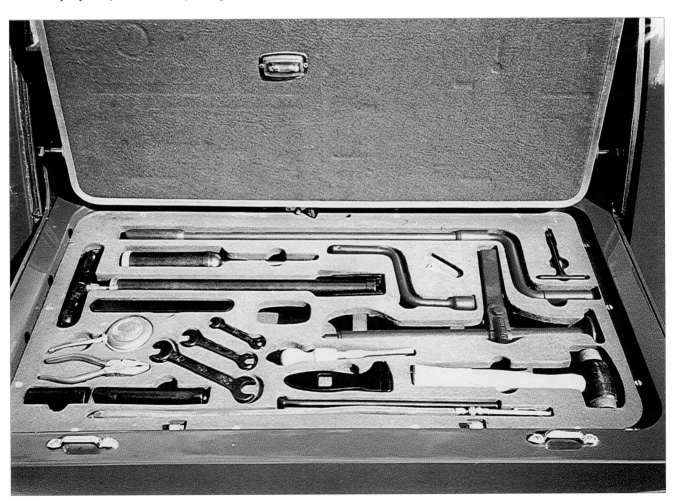

The Gossiper

● Frank Mullard (above): Once the proud owner of the distinctive 3.5 Jag (right) and below pictured at a classic car rally.

No ifs or Buts, Frank loved it

by **Pat Nurse**

WHEN Frank Mullard saw the 3.5 litre Jaguar car in 1959 he set his heart on having it and his wife Peggy supported him all the way.

The car was for sale at secondhand car salesman Mr Longmate's yard, at the back of the former Whitton's Bar on St Mary's Street, Lincoln. But there was a problem.

A deposit was needed on the 20-year-old car which cost the princely sum of £65 to buy outright.

"Frank earned £13 a week at that time and he gave me £10 for housekeeping," Peggy recalled.

"After he handed the money over he kept looking at me and then said he'd seen this car, it was a wonderful thing and he really wanted it. He was absolutely car mad, and this was to be his first car.

"I looked in the pantry and saw that we had plenty of eggs, six tins of beans and a bag of potatoes so I gave him the £10 back and we lived on egg and chips for the rest of the week.

"The car took us to the seaside every Sunday and we felt like a king and queen as we drove around. There were no seats in the back so we put in a cot mattress for our children to sit on."

The car, which did between 10 and 15 miles to to gallon, was hugely expensive to run in those days and a couple of years later when petrol rose from 4s 3d (21½p) to 4s 9d (24p) the family couldn't justify keeping it anymore.

Reluctantly they sold it, but they never forgot it or its distinguishing registration plate "But 7".

"We didn't see it again until three years ago when we were at a vintage car rally," Peggy, from Branston Booths, said.

"As soon as we got there I saw it and pointed out to Frank that his But 7 was there.

"He couldn't believe it. It was like being reunited with a long-lost child.

"We waited and waited for the owner, but nobody came all day.

"At another car rally we found out that the person who owned it lived just down the road from us, at Washingborough.

"Frank told him he used to own it and the man said he knew because Frank's name was still on the log book."

Sadly, Frank died just before Christmas last year and the car brings back fond memories of him for the family.

They spotted it in Echo Week a few weeks ago and learned it is now in the hands of the Lincolnshire Road Transport Museum at Whisby.

'No ifs or Buts, Frank loved it'
by Pat Nurse
Lincolnshire Echo, 23 May 1998
Reproduced with the kind permission of the Lincolnshire Echo

Motoring miscellany.
JOHN CHILD

'A Tale From The Heart' by No. 23
as told to Cyril Cooke
LVVS Newsletter – April 1995

During the Autumn of 1948, I, along with my seven sisters, was on the assembly line at Guy Motors. We were in build and would soon be delivered to Lincoln City Transport. The Lincoln depot was something of a Leyland stronghold, with its Lions and Titans in abundance, but we were confident we could meet the challenge as we already had ten wartime Arab sisters in there, and doing a damn fine job, so we were told.

I left Guy's factory in Wolverhampton just before my sisters and was sent down to London to be a 'star' at the Commercial Motor Show. They had fitted me with a Meadows six-cylinder engine and being special I was to show off. I didn't feel very special, more like the odd one out. On the stand at the show I came to like the attention and interest shown towards me, perhaps I was a 'star' of the show after all.

Well, having arrived at my new home at St Marks in Lincoln together with my sister No. 35 we went into service on 30th November 1948. We both had our photograph taken that first week and I posed beneath the Stonebow.

All the family of eight of us were in service within a week and we soon got to know Lincoln and the routes we were to work. Some of these routes were to uphill districts with my sisters coping well with the loads they carried. Their Gardner engines seemed ideally suited to the task, yet I seemed to labour heavily at times. The workshop gang were a friendly lot and they could see I struggled when heavily loaded so, from the age of five, I was put onto schedules with somewhat lighter loadings. I didn't care for this arrangement very much but it didn't last for long as I was taken into the workshops and my Meadows motor was removed by the gang. They put a Leyland 8.6 motor into me, removed from a Titan whose fate it was to be scrapped.

Well I worked this damn engine into the ground and once more I was confined to the garage back wall. It seemed an odd thing to me to marry a Leyland motor to a Guy. A marriage that was doomed from the start. I was rather like Cinderella that couldn't go to the ball,

only I couldn't go into service, lacking not a dress but an engine.

Old Fred White, the Rolling Stock Superintendent, was my friend and ally. When top dogs in the office upstairs said get rid of that damn 23 bus there was Fred shouting back for me – 'no way, she's a Guy and she will keep yet, we'll make something of her'.

Fred's word was his bond and after about two years out of action he found a new lease of life for me. Ruston & Hornsby, the Lincoln Ironworks, were producing a six cylinder engine for dragline navvies and wished to try out one of these engines in a bus. Yes, you dear reader have figured it out, I was to be a guinea pig again but what the hell, it was better than being stuck in the gloomy garage all day and eventually hauled off to the scrap yard prematurely and against Fred's better wishes.

They packed me off to Ruston's Boultham works in early 1960 and performed major surgery on me. Fitted with a RUSTON 6YDA AIR-COOLED engine I was duly returned to the St Marks depot, whereupon I entered the paint shop for a full repaint. When I re-entered service I once again felt rather special and had many photos taken in action. Every now and then Ruston's team of fitters would come back and check me over. Each time I passed with flying colours, it was great to be back in service and part of the fleet again.

After a few weeks a problem arose where only a few crews would take me out because I was too noisy, too hot in the cab and they said I vibrated too much. Well this was so, and all due to the colossal power I now possessed beneath my bonnet. Power so great I could now ascend Lindum Hill in top gear with a full standing load from Silver Street if I got a clear run through the traffic lights. I became a part-time service bus again and served in this capacity until 1967.

Two of my sisters had already retired back in '65 when they were displaced by a new breed of bus, the Atlantean. The rest of us were thrown out when the first of the single-deck Panthers arrived. I had the good fortune to be saved from the breakers yard by a group known as the Lincolnshire Vintage Vehicle Society. I had met some of the members and their vehicles on occasion.

Some of the bus fraternity of this group were reputed to be eccentric jealous characters, and I soon found this to be true when I moved to my new home at Whisby Road; for there in one thousand and one pieces was a Leyland Titan undergoing a rebuild by the joiner extraordinaire known as Cyril, accompanied by a few other enthusiastic characters. He wouldn't be tearing me apart as I was steel-framed and I didn't need surgery!

Well the years have rolled by, and I have now been in care for longer than I was in service with LCT. I was the fourth decker to join the throng here at Whisby Road and many have arrived since. I have seen some changes in that time, the biggest being the demolition of the utility shed and the building of a super structure to form an exhibition hall of some enormity.

I no longer have to lay up in the back shed with the wind blowing around one's private parts, or take my turn in the yard with the snow and rain running down my domes. All that bad weather took its toll on my exterior paintwork so the eccentrics have been at work and given me a super new coat of paint. My interior has had a jolly good clean up, my motor and brakes checked over, destination box winding gear has had minor surgery and last but not least the sign writer has applied his fine artwork, all going to stand me in good stead for many years to come, a show bus once again – old Fred would have been proud of me!

This article was written as a tribute to the late Mr Fred White, a former Vice-President of the Society. Due to his efforts we can be grateful for the co-operation obtained from Lincoln City Transport during the 1960/70s. Fred also gave his support to the safe acquisition of No. 23 when at one stage the bus was fixed to the tow bar of a recovery vehicle to be taken away for scrap, due to an administrative mix-up.

Facing page: No. 23 posed under 'The Stonebow' in Lincoln when new.
COURTESY OF LINCOLNSHIRE ECHO

The powerful but noisy air-cooled 'Ruston & Hornsby' engine.
LVVS COLLECTION

Three views of No. 23 parked up during a short outing for the photographer whilst at a Mersey and Calder Preservation Group rally at Meltham Mills in July 1994. Driver Steve Milner explained that lip-reading was a necessary attribute for conductors since conversation in the lower saloon was completely out of the question once the bus was on the move.
JOHN A SENIOR

'You'll Be Finished By Lunchtime'
On Location With The Tiger
by Bob Brewer
LVVS Newsletter – January 1996

About the middle of September Steve Milner got a phone call from John Beales – a self-employed property manager working for BBC TV.

They were filming in Norfolk for a three-part drama to be known as 'Over Here'. This is from the wartime saying about the Americans, 'overweight, oversexed and over here', so it had to be something connected with the American Forces.

He required a wartime single-decker and also a double-decker for one day's filming and the rate was very good. As it turned out we were not able to produce a double-decker at short notice so it was decided that Steve and I would go with the Leyland Tiger from the Museum.

The plan was to be on site by 8 o'clock on Sunday morning (this after an eighty odd mile drive in the Tiger) and 'you'll be finished by lunchtime'. We did get there by 8am – 'there' being the village of Castleacre, a few miles east of Swaffham and well off the beaten track. We were met by John Beales who immediately organised some stickers to cover the 'Lincolnshire' logos on the bus, some green paper over the adverts and a Swaffham 10A destination, all these incidentally stuck on with Vaseline. When this was done another chap came round with a bucket of black emulsion mixed with Fairy Liquid that they use to cover the white lines on the road, and flicked it all over the front of the Tiger.

We were then pointed in the direction of the catering vans where a full breakfast was available. I had just started mine when I was called to the wardrobe department in the Village Hall and given a bus driver's uniform complete with hat, shoes, shirt and tie. The reason I got the short straw being that I am a little older than Steve (although I don't know how they knew that) and all the younger men would be away at the war, they said.

Shortly afterwards I was given a two-way radio and introduced to a small but extremely vociferous young lady named Melanie, who was the Producer, and we commenced filming.

The procedure was to get everyone in place; I had three lady passengers in period costume and a conductress, Penny, and had to wait a little way up the village street. Melanie positioned various extras and vehicles around and when she was satisfied with everything would shout, 'quiet please, everyone very quiet, turn over and action – go, bus, go'. At which point the Tiger would lurch forward about twenty yards to the bus stop, passengers would get on and off, and then I would disappear out of range of the camera until I heard 'CUT' over the radio, at which point we stopped until the word came 'RESET', then I would reverse down the street to do it all again.

Preparing the Tiger for its stint on location.
STEVE MILNER

This went on for most of the morning until it started to rain, then we sat around waiting. At one o'clock lunch was announced and the weather immediately turned better. At two o'clock, having had lunch, we had a variation, with me driving away from the camera and meeting a jeep with five passengers on a blind bend. This proved to be fairly interesting once or twice but the rain soon put a stop to things again.

We sat around until six-thirty when they decided to call it a day, and could we please go back on Wednesday?

Wednesday was a late start for us so we arrived on site about twelve-thirty, ready for lunch, to find the village deserted, no vehicles, no catering vans or staff; only a few extras sitting in the pub. We managed to find out that there had been a change of plan, all the film crew had moved to West Raynham airfield where they were doing some inside shots of a B17, as featured in the film 'Memphis Belle'. This was top priority, not because it was costing £3,000 per hour, but because it had to be somewhere else the next day. We managed to get tickets for a free lunch in one of the local pubs and while we were eating this John Beales arrived full of apologies plus a cheque for the day's attendance; the only snag being the bus was required for filming the next day. Steve had to be at work but I provisionally agreed to take it after declining John's offer of a night in a hotel, deciding that this would not be well received back home. Back at the Museum Paul was regaled with tales of free food and drink and agreed to take a day off to keep me company. So at five o'clock the next morning it was back down the A17 again.

Thursday's filming was a bit more interesting. It entailed driving straight for the camera down the centre of the road and then veering right at the last minute, 'and don't slow down or stop 'til I shout', and this, in the village street, was very exciting.

This went on, plus some 'sound shots' until about two-thirty without a break when all of a sudden it was lunchtime and the filming was over. So we were 'finished by lunchtime'. Only the long drag home and back to the real world.

Altogether it was a very interesting experience with some nice people to work with, and very profitable for the Society. There was a good selection of vehicles on hire, some of them having been there for seven weeks. Among the military vehicles I saw two Bedford O Y's, an Austin K2, a Hillman Utility, a Jeep and a Morris C8 towing a gun. Civilian vehicles included an Austin 7 van, and most interestingly, two 1930s open tourers – a Delage and a Frazer-Nash. These two belonged to a lady living in the village, a member of the Guinness family, who had been given them – one for her 18th birthday and one for her 21st. The Delage was a non-runner and the Frazer-Nash would barely run, having to be push started every time, but I did see her driving it on Thursday morning, arriving on the site with a dog sitting on her lap.

The odd shower of rain added to the ambience.
STEVE MILNER

Above, the all-important Catering Team.
JOHN CHILD

Society members at work at the Easter 2001 Open Day.

Right, conductress Debbie Mole.
JOHN CHILD

Two examples of vehicle signwriting from a bygone age.
JOHN CHILD

'Lincoln's Centenary'
by Andy Izatt

First published in Bus & Coach Preservation, June 2004.

Bus & Coach Preservation magazine is available from all good newsagents.

Subscription enquiries on 02392 655224

Lincoln's Centenary

The Lincolnshire Vintage Vehicle Society turned out an impressive range of vehicles on Easter Sunday to mark the centenary of the start of municipal transport in Lincoln. ANDY IZATT went along to sample what was on offer

As we move through the first decade of the new millennium there are a growing number of centenaries to celebrate. The early years of the 20th century were peppered by the pioneering efforts of municipal authorities to establish public transport in towns and cities across the country. Lincoln was no exception with the Corporation buying the horse-drawn trams of the Lincoln Tramways Company in July 1904.

Centre of excellence

What marks the city out as unusual is that it has also been a centre of preservation excellence for almost half that time through the LVVS which celebrates 45 years this year. Thus its small, expertly maintained and active collection contains vehicles of an age and range that are rarely found elsewhere. Visitors to the Easter Sunday running day were not disappointed by the choice on offer which included all five of the Lincoln municipal vehicles currently running in preservation.

As well as being a charity, LVVS has become a limited company and the museum has 'Registered Museum' status. Of around 180 members some 60 are actively involved and Chairman Steve Milner emphasises that one of the group's strengths is that it draws on the expertise of people with interest in all types of historic vehicle. It was a point evident at the running day. As well as being able to travel on a wide range of vehicles of local interest, a rare visiting 1949

East Kent Dennis Lancet and Crosville RELH, there was the opportunity to sample the museum's own 1931 Chevrolet LQ 14-seater and a splendid selection of cars including a

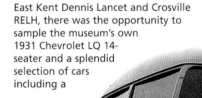

mayoral limousine. More cars — the museum has 20 — and commercials were on display as well as buses including the unique 1930 Bradford Leyland Badger.

Nothing stands still at the museum and LVVS is pursuing a £250,000 lottery grant that would contribute towards a £400,000 extension enclosing the space that is currently open between the main exhibition building and the workshop behind. As far as vehicles are concerned work continues on the restoration of FHN 833, a 1940 Bristol L5G, which has gained new brake linings and shackle pins and will shortly receive professional work on the boot framework, courtesy of a Lincolnshire County Council Heritage Grant. Three

Opposite above: Lincoln No5, the Applewhite-bodied Leyland Lion LT1 which is the very embodiment of 1920 style and refinement.
Pictures: ANDY IZATT

Opposite: Lined up to commemorate the centenary of the start of municipal public transport in Lincoln.

Above: Both the TD7 and PD2/41 participated in the afternoon photographers' tour, here in Brant Road.

Above right: 1961 Leyland Titan PD2/41 no89 follows no64, the TD7 20 years its senior as they turn into High Street from St Mark's.

buses that will hopefully be running at events later in the year are Lincolnshire Bristol K6A DBE 187, OHK 432, the well-known Colchester Roberts-bodied Daimler CVD6 and Eastern Counties HPW 133, a 1949 Bristol K5G that looks particularly smart after a recent repaint.

Lincoln at 100

The efforts of the LVVS are all the more valuable because there are few reminders of municipal transport in Lincoln although Lincolnshire RoadCar's city-based buses still use the

Lincoln City Transport name. The City Council sold its bus company to a Transport Act-inspired management employee buyout in November 1991. Despite Derby City Transport taking a 40% share the new company struggled. On the point of going into administrative receivership it was taken over by Traction Group-subsidiary, RoadCar in February 1993, ceasing to be a separate legal entity four years later. Municipal garages in Burton Road and St Marks were demolished in 2001 and 2002 with the later making way for retail development and student accommodation. Only the former tram depot remains standing.

At its height in the post deregulation era, standalone Lincoln City Transport operated over 100 vehicles including competitive minibus operations in Gainsborough and Scunthorpe as it expanded in a vain attempt to survive. But the company is perhaps best remembered for its 'Limo' door-to-door services to the Birchwood Estate and North Hykeham that used a fleet of 20 London-style FX4 taxis to counteract competition from RoadCar.

Operating in a regulated world, Lincoln City's predecessor, Lincoln Corporation Transport was a much more stayed affair running just 68 vehicles at the height of the early 1950s post war boom. It had introduced eight electric trams in 1905, notable not least because electric transport is to return to the city 99 years later in the form of a battery-powered Renault Master minibus that will operate up Steep Hill to the Cathedral from June.

The first buses were 32-seat Dennis CABs with bodywork by Thompson of Louth which entered service in 1920. Seven years later the municipal bought the first production Leyland Titan TD1 which gave 23 years service and also added Leyland Lion and Thornycroft single-deckers. Trams ceased in 1929 on receipt of more Titans that through various model evolutions became something of a fleet standard until 1967. Other types included Guy Arabs in the 1940s, AEC Bridgemasters, Leyland Atlanteans and from the 1970s, Bristol VRTs.

Like many of its contemporaries faced with falling patronage and rising costs, Lincoln introduced one-man-operation to its single-decker Leyland Tiger Cubs, later buying Panthers towards the end of the 1960s and Bristol REs with unusual Alexander bodywork in the 1970s. Autofare ticketing from 1971 underlined the decline in passenger numbers and the last conductors and crew-operated buses finished six years later.

The survivors

Despite the migration of a Roe-bodied Leyland PD2/41 to Belgium after withdrawal in 1977, most of the surviving Lincoln municipal buses have stayed closer to home. A number of East Lancs-bodied Bristol VRTs had survived because their 86-seat capacity made them ideal school buses but pairs with First Northampton and

Above: Lincoln Cathedral provides the backdrop for newly repainted 1941 Titan TD7 no64 and no89, the PD2/41 that is 20 years its junior.

Right: No23 (DFE 383) the Ruston & Hornsby-engined Guy Arab III with Guy/Park Royal bodywork awaits passengers outside Lincoln railway station.

Opposite above: Titans from very different Lincoln eras. No89 (RFE 416) with Fowler's CJN 441C, the onetime Lincoln City Transport training bus.

Opposite below: A fitting tribute from Lincolnshire RoadCar, Leyland Olympian no653 finished in 1920s Corporation livery.

Cedar Coaches of Bedford have now gone. First Devon & Cornwall took the Northampton buses for their engines while the Cedar vehicles passed to Abus in Bristol. The only one of these remaining in service, but smartly turned out is Dickinsons of Wrangle NFW 36V, usually used on a Stickney schools work. The Lincolnshire family firm still owns withdrawn UFW 39W.

Lincolnshire RoadCar continues to operate East Lancs-bodied DFW 42X, the very first long-wheelbase Leyland Olympian to be built, as well as KTL 43-45Y and later C46-48 KBE with semi-coach East Lancs bodywork. Four semi-coach East Lancs-bodied Volvo Citybuses new in 1988 continue to run for sister Traction Group company, Yorkshire Traction.

The three Lincoln buses in preservation that were not at the running day are all single-deckers currently undergoing restoration. Oldest is no41 (EVL 549E), one of 25 Roe-bodied Leyland Panthers delivered between 1967 and 1970 and owned by LVVS member Cyril Cooke. No73 (UVL 873M) is a 1973 Alexander-

bodied Bristol RELL6L that was donated to the LVVS in 2000 by Craig Tilsley. As previously reported in B&CP, no73's restoration will be extensive and this has now commenced away from the museum. No53 (UFX 718, *EPM 136V*) is the newest of the three, being one of five former Green Line AEC Reliances bought by Lincoln in 1986. The coach entered preservation in 2001 and is currently owned by LVVS member Peter Davis.

Flying the crest

On the day, all the Lincoln vehicles that could be running were out carrying passengers. At a respectable 75 years of age, they don't come any more impressive than no5 (VL 1263), an Applewhite-bodied Leyland Lion LT1, the first vehicle owned by LVVS. It made three trips with capacity loads every time.

Equally popular was no64 (BFE 419), a 1941 Roe-bodied Leyland Titan TD7 which has just been repainted in 1950s livery by Lincolnshire RoadCar thanks to a County Council Heritage Grant. No64 had been bought for preservation by LVVS founder member Vincent LeTall, subsequently passing to the society. Driven with considerable spirit by Andy Colley, the TD7's three outings included a very popular

photographers' tour in the company of no89 (RFE 416), a 1961 Leyland PD2/41, also a regular performer throughout the day on the service to the city centre. One of Lincoln's last conductor-operated buses in 1977, no89, owned by Steve Milner, is finished in post 1963 livery.

Quite a different Titan is CJN 441C, a former Southend Corporation Transport Massey-bodied PD3/6 that was used by Lincoln City Transport as a driver training bus in the late 1980s and early 1990s.
Now owned by Andrew Fowler of Holbeach Drove-based W.H. Fowler and Sons, the bus was immaculately finished in the family firm's livery and made three lunchtime return trips on the Moorland Centre car park shuttle service.

Perhaps the most distinctive Lincoln vehicle is LVVS-owned no23 (DFE 383), the 1948 Guy Arab III with Guy/Park Royal bodywork that appeared at the Commercial Motor Show. Originally fitted with a Meadows engine, no23 received a Leyland unit in 1953 only to have that replaced by an experimental, locally-built Ruston & Hornsby air-cooled engine in 1961. It's still got it 43 years later and the deafening sound effects were in no way diminished by the sympathetic driving of Steve Colley.

Two other Lincoln-liveried vehicles were giving rides on the day, but were separated by 66 years; they could not have been more different. 1927 Leyland Lion PLSC1 KW 474 was new to Blythe & Berwick of Bradford before passing to West Yorkshire Road Car and later Jersey Motor Transport. Identical to Lincoln Corporation's own no1 (VL 300), this is how the LVVS has chosen to preserve the bus which has been with the society since 1959, it even donning an appropriate registration plate for photographs. In terms of technological development, Lincolnshire Road Car's 1993 Leyland Olympian/ Alexander no653 (L603 NOS) could not have been more different. Finished in 1920s Corporation livery to mark the Centenary, it made a very appropriate stable mate for KW 474 and the other Lincoln vehicles operating on the day.

Thanks

Thanks go to Chairman Steve Milner and LVVS members for a thoroughly enjoyable event. A particular thank you goes to Andy Colley for organising the Corporation line up at the beginning of the day and to Jonathan Bigwood whose excellent programme provided an invaluable source of information for this article◆

And Finally . . .

'Ten Society Members' – Anon   LVVS Newsletter - July / August 1982

Ten Society Members,
Working in a line,
One didn't like the work,
Then there were nine.

Nine Society Members,
Working extra late,
One went and overslept,
Then there were eight.

Eight Society Members,
Took a 'bus' to Devon,
One stayed overnight,
Leaving only seven.

Seven Society Members,
Got into a fix,
One got bogged down in the mud,
And then there were six.

Six Society Members,
Drove near a hive,
A 'swarm' of bees attacked one,
And then there were five.

Five Society Members,
Looking out the door,
The 'committee' didn't like one,
And then there were four.

Four Society Members,
Drinking cups of tea,
One said 'Let's down tools',
Then there were three.

Three Society Members,
Were feeling rather blue,
One said 'Lets have a strike',
Then there were two.

Two Society Members,
The 'funds' were nearly gone,
One simply walked out,
Leaving only one.

This Society Member,
Who was left alone,
Just locked up the building,
And then there were none.

Not to be taken seriously.

'ONO', the globetrotting Bristol, pictured here in a blizzard on the morning of the 2008 Easter Open Day. *ANDY COLLEY*